COVER POINT

Impressions of Leadership in Pakistan

COVER POINT

Impressions of Leadership in Pakistan

JAMSHEED MARKER

Preface by
Stanley Wolpert

OXFORD
UNIVERSITY PRESS

OXFORD
UNIVERSITY PRESS

Oxford University Press is a department of the University of Oxford.
It furthers the University's objective of excellence in research, scholarship,
and education by publishing worldwide. Oxford is a registered trade mark of
Oxford University Press in the UK and in certain other countries

Published in Pakistan by
Oxford University Press
No. 38, Sector 15, Korangi Industrial Area,
PO Box 8214, Karachi-74900, Pakistan

ISBN 978-0-19-070424-7

Typeset in Adobe Caslon Pro
Printed on 68gsm Offset Paper

Printed by Mas Printers, Karachi

To my brother
Khursheed (1925–2010)
Scientist and Entrepreneur.
Gentlest, most noble, courageous, and kindest of men,
whose friendship was warm and true, and
whose constant affection suffused our hearts.
He served his country for a lifetime
with dedication, honour, modesty, and devotion.
And
To the people of Pakistan, who have suffered so much,
and continue to do so.

Epigraph

History with its flickering lamp stumbles along the trail of the past, trying to reconstruct its scenes, to revive its echoes, and kindle with faint gleams the passion of former days. What is the worth of all this? The only guide to a man is his conscience; the only shield to his memory is the rectitude and sincerity of his actions. It is very imprudent to walk through life without this shield, because we are so often mocked by the failure of our hopes and the upsetting of our calculations; but with this shield, however the fates may play, we march always in the ranks of honour.

Winston Churchill
In his eulogy to Neville Chamberlain
House of Commons, 12 November 1940

Contents

Acknowledgements

To Arnaz, my beloved wife, who continues to care for me from beyond, as she has always done whilst together. Thank you my darling.

To Niloufer, adorable daughter, lovely companion, and caretaker.

To Minoo, my brother, and so much else.

To Aban, for the love and support.

To Ameena Saiyid, OBE, Managing Director, Oxford University Press. Her contribution to the quantum of literacy in Pakistan remains as considerable and undiminished as ever.

To Nadia Ghani, for her professional ability and tolerance in coping with my idiosyncrasies.

And to the staff of OUP Karachi that is among the finest publishers.

Preface

Ambassador Jamsheed Marker's *Cover Point* is a legacy of his lifetime in the diplomatic service of Pakistan, from his cricket fielding position, 'near enough to the wicket to follow the action around the stumps ... yet sufficiently distant for a general overview of the state of play'. Unlike his previously published book *Quiet Diplomacy: Memoirs of an Ambassador of Pakistan* (OUP 2010), which is a rich history of his many ambassadorial assignments, this work is mostly a series of sad 'impressions' of Pakistan's most powerful leaders.

With the exception of the incorruptible Quaid-i-Azam Muhammad Ali Jinnah and his Muslim League lieutenant Liaquat Ali Khan, all of Pakistan's most powerful leaders 'succumbed, in increasingly pernicious fashion, to the malign and pervasive influences of sycophancy and flattery'. Jinnah's tubercular lungs led to his demise little more than one year after Pakistan's birth; just a few years later [in 1951], Liaquat was assassinated as he started to address a public meeting in Rawalpindi. Said Akbar, Liaquat's assassin, was immediately shot dead by a police officer, and though the Scotland Yard investigated the first of Pakistan's many assassinations, the 'mystery' of Liaquat's 'death remains unsolved'.

Soon after Liaquat's demise, Pakistan's extensive series of martial coups began, the first major one led by Iskander Mirza and Ayub Khan. But 'two lions cannot live in the same cage', so Ayub sent Mirza packing off to London, where he and his wife occupied a modest flat off Exhibition Road, in which he sadly reported to Marker that others he once thought his 'friends' would 'now run a mile if they see me'.

Ayub's Martial Law Administration moved Pakistan's capital from Karachi to the newly built Islamabad, launching an era of economic boom, rapid growth, and development. Marker was sent from Ghana to Romania, but on returning home after the Indo-Pak War of 1965 he found 'disaffection' with Ayub sweeping the country, led by Zulfikar Ali Bhutto and Sheikh Mujibur Rahman. The once robust Field Marshal suffered a series of heart attacks, and had to undergo surgery in Texas for treatment. His Foreign Minister, Z. A. Bhutto, soon began to attack Ayub most vigorously after the Peace Treaty that he signed with India's Prime Minister, Lal Bahadur Shastri, in Tashkent in 1966. 'A battered and confused Ayub Khan' was 'compelled' to hand over his Martial Law powers to his chosen successor General Yahya Khan in 1969. Under Yahya, after nationwide elections were held, leading to a major victory for Sheikh Mujib and his Bengali Awami League, Pakistan lost the majority of its population following the defeat it suffered at the hands of India in the 1971 Indo-Pak War, leading to the birth of Bangladesh.

Thereafter, Pakistan lurched from one corrupt and mega-lomaniacal leader to another: first Z. A. Bhutto, whose 'actions and policies have done the most damage to Pakistan ... he drove the country into two wars and a messy breakup.' Bhutto was soon to be hanged by his own chosen COAS, General Zia ul-Haq, who resolved to impose 'an Islamic system' onto Pakistan's body politic. Zia introduced 'a series of draconian martial law regulations and punishments, including the barbaric system of public floggings.' In August of 1988, Zia's plane went down in the desert over Bahawalpur in Punjab shortly after taking off. All those on board, including Zia and the US Ambassador Arnold Raphel, were killed. 'Leadership in Pakistan possesses occupational hazards,' Marker concludes in a chapter.

'What took Pakistan from its turbulent but pristine formation in 1947 to its present condition?' Marker asks at the end of his long, clear view of Pakistan from his *cover point*. 'I am quite certain that its founder ... Jinnah would find it difficult to recognize, much less accept, the country in its present form.'

Stanley Wolpert

Recollections and Reflections

Reason and judgement are the qualities of a leader

Publius Cornelius Tacitus

This above all: to thine own self be true,
And it must follow, as the night the day,
Thou canst not then be false to any man.

Hamlet, William Shakespeare

Although I had attained some international status as a Test Cricket commentator, on the field itself my performance at the game fluctuated between the mediocre and the dismal. The result was that I never made it into any good team, my major achievement being chosen as Captain of the Jaipur House XI at the Doon School, Dehradun, India. It was in this capacity that I realized that cover point was quite a good position in which to field: it was near enough to the wicket to follow the immediate action around the stumps and yet sufficiently distant for a general overview of the state of play. The similarity between the observation point on the cricket field and the positions in which I later found myself in the real world suggested the title of this book.

My career as a diplomat brought me into contact with political leaders all over the world, which in turn nurtured a fascination with the manner of exercise of power and leadership. Some of this has been reported in my memoirs, and deals mostly with foreign personalities. In the present instance, I have attempted to record impressions of the Pakistani leaders whom I have been privileged to know and serve. And I do so from my fielding position of cover point. I got closer to some leaders than I did to others; admired some more than others. This stemmed from the opportunity that I had to observe, from a reasonable distance, not only the methods and styles of work and policy decisions made by political leaders, but also the strengths in their personal character, such as patriotism, intelligence, foresight, and courage, as well as the foibles in their personal traits, including amorality, arrogance (both personal and messianic), and venality. An observation which I found to be particularly compelling was the manner in which even the strongest-willed leaders succumbed, in increasingly pernicious fashion, to the malign and pervasive influences of sycophancy and flattery. The distinguished British military historian Captain B. H. Liddell Hart has said, 'The barrier of rank is the highest of all barriers in the way of access to truth'. Time and again, the newly installed leader became increasingly intolerant of advice, however impartial, well-intended, and sincerely tendered. Moreover, they almost inevitably created a coterie of courtiers who should have been advisers; and worse still, of advisers turned into courtiers. These conditions provide the ready link to corruption, an evil for which flattery provides the sugar-coating. This fearful combination of sycophancy and corruption has throughout history been a common phenomenon in many lands, and is by no means unique to

Pakistan. But over a period of time, other political systems have developed institutions designed to maintain checks and balances in the exercise of political power. This in turn has led not only to the creation of mature political leadership but, more importantly, to a universally accepted concept of probity in the conduct of public affairs. Unfortunately, such a stable and satisfactory situation, which is the *sine qua non* of a genuine democracy, has not occurred during most of Pakistan's history. With the exemplary notable exception of M. A. Jinnah, and that of his successor Liaquat Ali Khan, power has been acquired through usurpation in one form or another, whether by outright military intervention, palace intrigues and coups, or manipulated electoral processes. Of further concern is the fact that, at the moment of usurpation of power, there has been a general public acceptance of the action, particularly in its immediate aftermath. The fact that this acceptance has been short-lived, and has evaporated soon after the event, is also a part of the political tragedy of Pakistan. In this connection, I recall the cynical observation of a friend, who is as patriotic as he is intelligent, that we are a nation of sheep led by wolves.

At the end of the century, the Second Communist International Annual Conference was held in Brussels and broke up in disarray. It was in a room, filled with heavy fumes from stale cigarette smoke, half-empty glasses of cognac and liquor, and laden with deep, bitter personal animosities. One of the participants was the Russian Prince Pyotr Kropotkin, founder of the Anarchist Communism Movement. Surveying, with regret and disdain, the disorder and acrimony that the delegates had brought to the Conference, Kropotkin said, 'Alas, comrades, we are not the doctors, we are the disease'.

The past century has been one of the most eventful and turbulent in the history of the world. About halfway through its duration, following two global wars, there emerged a huge expansion in the number of nation-states, from about 54 to 192. Pakistan was among the earliest nova in this political cosmological explosion. The book is an attempt to report what I witnessed of those early exciting and tumultuous days, and to record my impressions of the leaders who guided the country, shortly before and during the early years of its formation. It has not been an easy task, for memory plays tricks, and recollection is often distracted by the insidious gravitational pulls of afterthought.

The reader is urged to view this book as neither history nor biography nor memorabilia. It is simply a series of sketches illustrated from my personal observations, in a lifetime covering almost a century, of the persons who appeared on the landscape of Pakistan during that period. It is a superficial book, in the truest sense of the word, consisting as it does of a compendium of highly subjective recollections that is bound to evoke controversy, perhaps even sensation. But it is not written for that purpose. After having observed the state of affairs for a long period of time, I have made an attempt to ask and find answers to questions that have agitated my mind, and the minds of so many others. What took Pakistan from its turbulent but pristine formation in 1947 to its present condition? I am quite certain that its founder, Muhammad Ali Jinnah, would find it difficult to recognize, much less accept, the country in its present form. There are so few of us left who have lived through and remember the old days. And we are steadily getting fewer.

True, it was the urge for power that motivated the actions of all of our leaders, and once they had achieved office, they were all exposed to the same destructive elements of greed, pride, and feelings of infallibility, each of these defects being fuelled by flattery and sycophancy, finally leading to corruption. The sole and outstanding exceptions were Muhammad Ali Jinnah and Liaquat Ali Khan. Their only fault was that they did not live long enough and left us too early: Jinnah in 1948 and Liaquat in 1951. The often expressed criticism of army interventions in the affairs of the country is entirely justified. But its validity is circumscribed by the equally compelling fact that army action has always been provoked by failure or near breakdown in the political system, and its intervention has generally been welcomed. The army has maintained its position as the only stable institution in the country. As the politicians clearly and dismally failed to establish a civilized political system, from time to time the dogs of war have leapt out of their kennels. I have been a sickened witness to this phenomenon more frequently than I care to recall.

Whilst reviewing the roles of the Pakistani leaders with whom I have had associations or contacts, I felt that the general impression and assessments hitherto prevalent needed correction. In some cases (e.g. Zia ul-Haq) there had not been sufficient public recognition of achievements, whilst in other instances (e.g. Z. A. Bhutto), there is need for substantial de-Stalinization. Judgement on this sensitive issue is of course left to the reader. There is a wide choice of both saints and sinners, not to mention a blending of the two.

In writing this book, the first and most important disclaimer is to assert that it is neither history nor biography. The approach and treatment are much too perfunctory and desultory for such serious and important fields of knowledge and learning. Nor can it be correctly described as a memoir, since none of the incidents or conversations mentioned in the book were either noted or diarized at the time when they occurred. It is merely a compendium of recollections and reflections spanning almost a century, of one who has seen something of the world and who, through the mists and shadows of time, puts his recall into words. I do this seated at a word processor and listening to the glorious creations of Beethoven, Bach, Mozart, and Sufi Ustad Nusrat.

My gratitude goes out to Arnaz, my darling wife, and Niloufer, my beloved daughter, without whose support and understanding neither this book nor anything else in life could have been possible. I also wish to thank my brother Minoo, who has been my friend, counsellor, and companion throughout our lives. His devotion and affection has sustained me in my moments of distress and enlivened me in my moments of happiness. Above all, we share a particular and peculiar sense of humour that the rest of the world finds odd. And of course there is Sam, whose intelligent and quiet encouragement has been the steadfast element in our lives. I owe him more than can ever be expressed.

In the course of writing this book, I have constantly been reminded of the immortal exhortation of the Greek philosopher Parmenides of Elea: 'Heed not the blind eye, the echoing ear, nor yet the tongue; But bring to this great debate the test of reason'.

Finally, all errors and omissions in this book are my own.

Jamsheed Marker
2015

Prologue

The Quetta Club: Midnight of 13–14 August 1947, and a roaring party going on in celebration of the independence of Pakistan and India.

Quetta, which until then was one of the major garrison cities of the hitherto mighty British Empire, had been comparatively immune from the political winds that had buffeted the Indian subcontinent; an isolation which, in its own fashion, helped to limit the horrific violence and excesses that were even then exploding elsewhere in the region.

The independence celebration party at the club was a cheerful, boisterous affair—with plenty of food and drink for the members and their guests. The premises were decked out in a profusion of small paper flags of the emerging Dominions of Pakistan and India fluttering alongside each other in amity, with a smattering of Union Jacks to embellish the cordiality. The joyful Indians and Pakistanis of the newly created Pakistan were in a euphoric state. So many of us had waited for so many years for this glorious day; we could not quite believe that we were now at last free citizens. Although India still had twenty-four hours to wait for its independence, Pakistan was free.

The charged atmosphere of that evening remains etched in my memory forever. The British, of whom there were a great number at the party, were almost as emotional as us, though perhaps for different reasons. Some, the wartime army officers, were just glad to be going home, but others, the army, civil, and police officers who, like their ancestors, had spent a lifetime in the subcontinent, were clearly beset by a touch of *schadenfreude*.

But even as we were celebrating, I knew that in other parts of the country a wave of violence and killings had commenced; that terror stalked the land; and that the jollity at the Quetta Club was artificial, utterly removed from the grim realities of the birth pangs of Pakistan and India. I recalled Charles Dickens' memorable description of an earlier turbulent era: 'It was the best of times, it was the worst of times. ... It was the spring of hope, it was the winter of despair'. A very heavy price was being paid for independence, but despite that, there were no signs of despair, even though we knew that we were in the process of making the first substantial payment for our freedom. On the contrary, the country was filled with enthusiastic optimism and pride. We were determined to make our Pakistan a great nation.

At the Quetta Club that evening, there were speeches which extolled the ideals of the British, the Indians, and the Pakistanis. There was recall of the many friendships forged in the Second World War that had recently concluded (1945), and promises were made for their continuation in the future. After the British and Indian representatives, who were of course army officers, had spoken, it was the turn of 'the senior most Pakistani officer'. That officer happened to be Major Agha Mohammed Yahya Khan.

1

The Early Days

Liberty is not a means to a higher political end.
It is itself the highest political end.

Lord Acton—Bridgworth Lecture

The creation of Pakistan was a manifestation of the vision, dedication, and determination of Muhammad Ali Jinnah, and the popular will of the millions who followed him, supported him, and believed in him. His successor, Liaquat Ali Khan, already in office as Prime Minister, assumed power through an established constitutional process following the early and tragic death of Jinnah on 11 September 1948. This was perhaps the only occasion in the history of Pakistan when succession in leadership was conducted under recognized norms. After the assassination of Liaquat, however, a deleterious pattern was established whereby power was acquired through usurpation in the paradox, already stated, of popular acceptance of changes of regime, even those generated by military coups.

The independence of Pakistan and India (in chronological sequence) in 1947, after two hundred years of British rule, marked a watershed in history. It triggered an era of decolonization all over the world, with the systematic dismantling of the colonies of the European powers:

British, French, Dutch, German, Italian, Spanish, and Portuguese. The legitimate claim that 'the sun never sets on the British Empire' (we used to joke in our college days that this was because God did not trust the Englishman in the dark) rapidly lost validity following the independence of Pakistan and India, as country after country in Asia and Africa attained freedom. In many instances, the transition to independence was comparatively smooth, but in other cases, there was turbulence and lasting discord. None could have engendered more violence and cruelty than that which occurred in the Indian subcontinent, where millions were killed, often in the most barbaric fashion. Mass migrations took place on a scale that was unprecedented. The discord, being of tectonic political proportions, sadly, but not unsurprisingly, continues to this day. Through the summer and autumn of 1947, as the subcontinent struggled and thrashed its way in the throes of independence, I found myself caught up in the frenzy of those events: would there really be a Pakistan? and if so, what would it comprise and look like? How would the two Dominions live separately and yet work together? Above all, how would we, particularly in Pakistan, find an end to the killings and chaos, bring about law and order, and establish a government?

My service in the Royal Indian Navy had ended with the conclusion of World War II whilst I was in Bombay (Mumbai), where I was posted to the Naval and Civil Selection Boards, and was also involved in the arrangements that followed the settlement of the Indian Naval Mutiny.

This event is not much remembered these days, but was, at the time, a shot across the bows, a symbolic signal of the end of the British Empire in India.

Those of us who lived through those momentous times—and we are getting fewer by the day—each have our own recollections, most of them unforgettably painful and unrecorded. Khushwant Singh's *Train to Pakistan*, and Sa'adat Hasan Manto's *Black Milk*, written shortly after these events, are perhaps the most moving and powerful descriptions of that epochal era. As I cast my mind back, I marvel at the good fortune and circumstances that shielded me from the atrocities and horrors that affected so many others. Although communal riots occurred on a nationwide scale, the worst affected areas were Bihar and the Punjab. I was never in Bihar during those times, and was never exposed to any of the atrocities in the Punjab, even though I met many of the victims—Hindus, Muslims, and Sikhs—and heard their tales of horrors. In the India of those times, war and peace appeared to live alongside each other, with mayhem in one part of the country and normalcy in most others. At the time when passengers were being mercilessly butchered in the carriages of the North Western Railway in the Punjab, I was able to have tea, toast, and sandwiches in the Deccan Queen of the Great Indian Peninsular Railway as it traversed the Western Ghats between Bombay and Poona. Civil air transport had been established after World War II, and I recollect being able to travel in sturdy Dakotas, for both business and pleasure, between the major cities of India—Karachi, Bombay,

Quetta, New Delhi, Lahore, and Secunderabad. The two Dominions were in a state of flux, but in the course of time restrictions on movement had became perceptibly more irksome as the bureaucracy of Partition increased its hold. But it was an incident during the brief period when subcontinental peripatetic activity was still possible that provided me with a vivid recollection of the epoch. I was at a cocktail party on the green, manicured lawns of the elegant New Delhi Gymkhana where, to the tinkling of ice in whisky glasses, the topic of conversation was whether Pakistan would last for three months or six months. My remonstrations were met with polite but barely concealed condescension. On my return to Karachi the next day, as I drove past the Cantonment Railway Station (simply known as Cantt Station) on my way home, I saw a large number of goods wagons with their doors open, and men seated on wooden boxes working on the bundles of official files which were stacked around them. Government offices were not yet ready, so these dedicated civil servants, officers, and clerks, determined to ensure that the work of the state must go on, were attending to the papers as soon as the documents arrived from New Delhi. The outside temperature was 102 degrees Fahrenheit. This, I thought to myself, was truly the Pakistan of Muhammad Ali Jinnah: indomitable, defiant, dedicated, and motivated. The country would surely last more than three months.

In the New Delhi that I had just left, the imposing edifices of Lutyens' North and South Blocks maintained their sanguine existence: housing offices, desks, chairs, and papers that continued the working of government in familiar and unhindered surroundings. Only the occupants had changed, with the Indians now moving smoothly into the rooms hitherto occupied by Britons. In Karachi, on the other hand, it was a total scramble. A neat, compact provincial city, comprising of a population of three hundred and fifty thousand, had suddenly been designated as the capital of a country of over a hundred million! An entirely new government and administration was being set up from scratch. The process of governance had to be continued and yet re-established; affairs of state conducted; law and order maintained; accommodation found for ministers, bureaucrats, and clerks, for embassies and business houses that were flocking to the newly established state. (In the search for accommodation, my family residence was requisitioned and we were obliged to find another house.) It was truly one massive ad hoc operation. M. H. Zuberi, an ICS (Indian Civil Service) officer with a distinguished record of service in India and then in Pakistan, has a vivid record of the dramatic and unsettled events of that period in his book, *Voyage through History* has written:

> On 15 August 1947 a telegram was received in the Ministry of Communications from the Maharaja of Kashmir asking for a standstill agreement on communications and transport, hitherto in operational force. I took it to Sardar Nishtar who could not hide his gleeful satisfaction and with a non-challant (*sic*) gesture of his hand told me 'send it to the Foreign Office'. Where is the Foreign Office? was my attempt to spring another surprise on him. We had not yet organized the Foreign Office, no building had yet

been earmarked and the Foreign Secretary, Ikramullah, was sharing a table with the Cabinet Secretary and was wasting his jokes on him. Nishtar later took the telegram to P. M. Liaquat Ali Khan and much was made of this telegram, confirmed with a letter, when Pakistan case was argued before the Security Council. We did not know then that the Maharaja had acted on Mountbatten's advice and had asked for a similar agreement with India.[*]

Thus, one day after its creation, the Dominion of Pakistan's Ministry of Foreign Affairs and its Cabinet Secretariat consisted of one shared desk from which its two occupants, brilliant and dedicated officers, dealt with the machinations of Mountbatten as they went about establishing the infrastructure of their respective Ministries. Working out of stuffy rooms, seated on makeshift furniture, this was their determined response to the cries of 'Pakistan Zindabad'! that floated out of the refugee camps all over Karachi.

Above all, there was the massive inflow of refugees that arrived in droves every day, filling Karachi with sad, run-down, overcrowded, and insanitary *bastis* (shanty towns). Uprooted from their ancestral homes in the most cruel fashion, they were faced with a future in which uncertainty was the only possible prediction. And yet, I recall frequently hearing, as I drove past these dwellings, spontaneous slogans of 'Pakistan Zindabad!' Such were the early heroic days of Pakistan, when the land was filled with hope, courage, and determination.

---

[*] Zuberi, M. H., *Voyage Through History*, vol. 1 (Karachi: Hamdard Foundation, 1987), 60.

The multifarious political and humanitarian problems that deluged the government could have crippled the most stable of administrations, let alone one that, in its fragile infancy, found itself in the bruised and buffeted city of Karachi in 1947–48. With the honourable exception of Bahawalpur, the accession of the Princely States to Pakistan had not been complete. Among the contiguous units, the rulers of Kalat and Kashmir were still hesitant, and while Jinnah was able to bring the former into the fold, the saga of Partition sparked in Kashmir a conflict that would dominate the South Asian subcontinent for the next sixty-two years. Meanwhile, Indian military action in Junagadh swiftly quelled a feeble, futile, and unjustified attempt by the Nawab to accede to Pakistan. (I recollect following the course of the one-sided military action in the newspapers. The Indian force was commanded by Commodore Ram Das Katari, a former shipmate and friend of mine in the Royal Indian Navy; the irony of it was a searing experience, but not uncommon to many of us at the time.) However, the issue of Hyderabad was very different, and the Nizam's moves to secure an independent state were followed with much excitement in Pakistan. The government appeared to provide the Nizam with unconcealed public political and diplomatic support, including helping the transfer of considerable funds from the State's treasury to London and facilitating the activities and movements of the leading members of the Nizam's cabinet. I vividly recall that Pakistan's press and radio were filled with news about Hyderabad, whereas comparatively less was being said about Kashmir; even though the Maharaja of Kashmir was displaying his obduracy, unrest in the state was already rampant. Moreover, disquiet on its border had already provoked military skirmishes. In the event, the Hyderabad issue was efficiently settled by Indian 'police action', and the State was duly dissolved and merged into Andhra Pradesh. But the issue of Kashmir still continues to burn.

My recollection of the time was that Hyderabad occupied so much more of the newspaper headlines than Kashmir that it has left me with the haunting thought that we were, somehow, blindsided by Hyderabad over Kashmir. Should we have concentrated more on removing the Maharaja and less on supporting the Nizam? And if we had succeeded in our efforts, would the end result be any different? Subsequent events render the idea purely speculative, of course. Records of the negotiations that took place at the time are now available and they depict some of the chicanery that took place in New Delhi during those days. The splendid accounts by two of the most able historians on the Indo-Pak subcontinent, Stanley Wolpert and H. M. Seervai, have indicated, with clinical clarity, the dubious activities associated with the Radcliffe Award, attributing culpability to Louis Mountbatten, Jawaharlal Nehru, and Cyril Radcliffe himself.

The unprecedented events in India and Pakistan in 1947 and 1948 moved with bewildering rapidity and fluidity. I had no access to any of the leadership at the time, shifting occupations from a low-level temporary position as a civil servant in the Home Department of the Government of India (I had been transferred from the Naval Selection

Board to the Civil Selection Board) to a modest business
activity in the private sector. This obliged and enabled me
to travel in many areas of the newly created Dominions
and to interact with people of varying levels on the social
scale: friends, former colleagues now turned civil servants,
lawyers, businessmen, and above all, workers in our factories
and in other industries. I saw the agonies of Muslims who
fled India and Hindus who fled Pakistan; many of them
close friends of mine and of each other. It soon became
clear that mass violence perpetrated with incomprehensible
cruelty had added a grim reality to the alteration of the
subcontinent just as much as the political arrangement
messily cobbled together in New Delhi. Jinnah's idea and
hope that Hindus would continue to live in Pakistan and
Muslims in India never really got off the ground. I was too
much of a nonentity to be present in the august chamber on
11 August 1947 and was only able to hear Jinnah's famous
speech to the Constituent Assembly of Pakistan on a
scratchy radio recording, and read about it in the next day's
newspapers. Even after over six decades, it reverberates in
my mind as when that clarion call was first sounded.

> If we want to make this great state of Pakistan happy and
> prosperous we should wholly and solely concentrate on the
> well-being of the people and especially of the masses and
> the poor. You are free—you are free to go to your temples,
> mosques or any other places of worship in this state of
> Pakistan. You may belong to any religion, caste or creed;
> that has nothing to do with the business of the state ... in
> due course of time Hindus will cease to become Hindus
> and Muslims will cease to be Muslims—not in a religious

sense for that is the faith of an individual—but in a political sense, as citizens of one state.

A few short, tumultuous months after his inspirational exhortation to the legislators and people of his country, on 11 September 1948, Muhammad Ali Jinnah, the founder and creator of Pakistan, passed away in an ambulance that had broken down on the road whilst it was conveying the desperately ill Governor General from Mauripur airport to his official residence. As Jinnah would have wished, and as was his custom, the public was not to be inconvenienced by his movements. Accordingly, on this last fateful journey, no roads were blocked or cut off. There were no sirens, no outriders, no armoured automobiles or jeeps, with flashing lights and carrying fierce looking men wielding automatic weapons as Jinnah's subsequent sleek pretenders resorted to, living a terrified, protected existence from the people they claimed to lead. In the chaotic days that followed Partition, Pakistan was scrambling to acquire its due assets and to restore crumbled resources. The latter included, in an act of supreme tragedy, a broken-down old military ambulance, bearing the heroic stricken man who had created Pakistan.

The news of Jinnah's death devastated Pakistan in the same overwhelming manner that had manifested itself at its creation just a few months before; but this time euphoria had been replaced by countrywide melancholia, tinged with anxiety. I attended a massive public condolence meeting held at the Residency in Quetta where the sorrowful, orderly crowd had overflowed from the grounds to the roads that converged onto the meeting place. They had

come from everywhere, not just Quetta, but from as far
away as Mastung, Sariab, Baleli, and even Chaman, in
solemn homage to a man they had never seen or heard, but
whom they revered beyond any other. There were speeches,
of course, but nobody really listened to them—each person
in that vast congregation seemed lost in his private, personal
grief. Fierce looking old men with huge beards and tear-
stained cheeks wept loudly, as others closed their eyes
and mumbled quiet prayers. As I walked back home from
the meeting with Nawab Sir Asadullah Khan Raisani, I
recollect mentioning the instinctive feeling that hitherto
Pakistan was Jinnah and Jinnah was Pakistan; people would
have to get used to thinking of a Pakistan without the
towering presence of an omniscient Jinnah. As I expressed
my youthful forebodings, the wise old Baloch patriarch
was sad, but unbowed, and charged with the determination
possessed by all Baloch leaders. 'He has completed his work
and given us a country. Now it is up to the Prime Minister
to run it. What else is there to do?' And this epitomized the
manner in which the people of Pakistan came to willingly
accept the orderly succession and transfer of power in the
country.

Following a brief, productive Cabinet Meeting, Khwaja
Nazimuddin, the respected senior political leader from
Bengal, assumed the office of Governor General, whilst
Liaquat Ali Khan continued as Prime Minister. Since
nobody could, in any way, realistically replace Jinnah, it
was understood that Nazimuddin would assume the titular
functions of Head of State while Liaquat would take

charge of the administration as Head of Government. The evolution was smooth and transparent, carried out by and involving political representatives of the highest stature, who had been the closest supporters of the Quaid-i-Azam in his struggle for Pakistan. I well recollect how we all accepted this transition, welcomed it, and were proud of the effortless manner in which it was accomplished. This was the first transfer of power in Pakistan, and was the only one that had the unanimous support of the people: sixty-two years later, they are still waiting for the next one, but there is little indication that a transfer of power in similar transparent fashion is likely to occur again.

I never had the privilege of meeting Quaid-i-Azam, which is one of the greatest regrets of my life. What little I learned about him came from the extensive literature that exists, particularly Ayesha Jalal's *The Sole Spokesman*, Stanley Wolpert's *Jinnah of Pakistan*, and of course the scholarly compilation of Jinnah's work by Dr Zawar Hussain Zaidi.

Over forty years after his death, I met Mr Jinnah's daughter, the vivacious and riveting Mrs Dina Wadia, in New York, and was immediately captivated by the forceful aura of her personality. Slim and petite, closely resembling her father, she exuded an air of confidence and regal dignity that could be so impressive as to sometimes intimidate people. But once one got to know her, as I had the great privilege and good fortune to do so, she was warm, gentle, considerate, and friendly. We talked about her illustrious father, whom she adored. These conversations remain confidential in deference to the understanding that she so generously reposed in me. Suffice it to say that she provided a vivid description not only of the frenetic visits to their home by the leading politicians of the time, but also their personalities, their strengths, their foibles, pettiness, and venality. Amongst all of this, her father stood unmoved and impeccable. The only event that I can report, which I do with considerable personal emotion, was Dina's account of a late night telephone call which she received from her father in New Delhi, at the conclusion of the arduous political negotiations. He exclaimed to her, 'Dina, we've got Pakistan!' It is sad and sobering to reflect that Dina has visited Pakistan only once. She does not believe, and quite rightly so, that it is the land that was envisioned by her father, Muhammad Ali Jinnah.

Meanwhile, the violence and turbulence continued, as the two newly constituted dominions began the search for their separate identities and for the means to establish them. Once again, the task appeared more difficult for Pakistan than it did for India, and for much the same reasons— for India, it was a matter of maintaining continuity; for Pakistan, an issue of creation. The Indians had to keep their administration, offices, businesses, and shops going as they coped with an influx of refugees from Pakistan, whereas in Pakistan, the task was not only to accommodate the homeless but to establish a whole new socio-economic fabric. A noteworthy element was the transfer of the burden of entrepreneurship from the Hindu traders, particularly the Marwaris and Sindhis who had fled to India from villages in Sindh and East Bengal, to the Memons and

Bohras from Gujarat and Kathiawar who replaced them, both in the rural economies of East and West Pakistan, as well as in the urban markets of Karachi, Lahore, and Dacca (Dhaka). In each Dominion, this enterprising community displayed its skill and initiative in a formidable display of adaptation: in Pakistan, by taking up the slack; in India, by application of fresh capital and skills. In subsequent years, the industrialists of Pakistan, with a clear field available and the support of an enthusiastic government, made an impressive contribution to the economic growth of the nation. In retrospect, it appears to me that through all the terrible turmoil and turbulence that convulsed the subcontinent during the period of Partition, it was perhaps the mercantile community on both sides that emerged as the most unscathed. Traders are adept as a species, and pragmatism is an effective survival skill.

The atmosphere that prevailed in the subcontinent in 1947–49 could truly be described as an interregnum, and one that will never be seen again. India and Pakistan were now two nations, but the separation was by no means complete, and there was an unrestricted movement of persons and goods between the two countries. I used to fly frequently between Karachi and Bombay on business and to meet family. I saw in Bombay an increasing number of automobiles with Karachi license plates—an indication of the freedom of movement and absence of restriction that prevailed at the time. But in the north and east of India, communal violence prevailed on a massive scale, and ominous signs of military confrontation between India and Pakistan over

Kashmir began to emerge. On the political scene, there was the dangerous deadlock brought about by the Indian government's decision to withhold Pakistan's share of the sterling reserves, thus turning a crisis situation in Pakistan into a financial disaster that threatened the existence of the state. Pakistan was literally on the verge of bankruptcy and was salvaged temporarily through a bold and generous act by the Nizam of Hyderabad. He transferred funds from his State's sterling reserves held in London to Pakistan.

But the outrageous nature of the Indian government's continued pressure tactics dismayed even Mahatma Gandhi, who decided to go on a fast seeking the release of Pakistan's legitimate dues. I was in Bombay at the time and saw the dramatic transformation in the public image and attention: a heated political dispute in which India had the upper hand over Pakistan had been suddenly transformed into a matter of keeping the Mahatma alive. Bulletins on his health replaced reports and statements on the financial stand-off. It was only when the Indian government relented and released Pakistan's legitimate dues that Gandhi broke his fast. A sense of relief manifested itself over most of the subcontinent. As I flew back to Karachi in a much more settled frame of mind, I did not know, like everybody else, that this would be Gandhi's last fast, perhaps the most noble of his many such acts. It had triggered his eventual assassination. When it occurred, I was again in Bombay, this time in a movie theatre. The film was interrupted by a bulletin flashed on the screen, and I remember praying and hoping that the assassin was not a Muslim.

By the year 1951, travel and commerce between the two dominions became increasingly restrictive. It was clear that I had to curtail my business activities in India and concentrate on them in Pakistan. Here, the people were engaged in the exciting process of nation building on the widest possible scale. The existing institutions, such as schools, colleges, hospitals, were energized and expanded, and new ones built. Roads and dwellings were constructed, and businesses, both commercial and industrial, were established. Factories that were coming into production helped in creating jobs and absorbing and integrating the immense refugee population.

A large proportion of the refugees comprised of helpless women, who, when they arrived in Pakistan, were even more destitute and penurious than their men folk. The amelioration of the plight of these unfortunate women was the immediate and greatest concern of Begum Ra'ana Liaquat Ali Khan, the dynamic and scintillating wife of Prime Minister Liaquat Ali Khan. As soon as she arrived in Karachi and moved into 10 Victoria Road (which used to be the official residence of the Collector Karachi but then became the Prime Minister's House) she established the All-Pakistan Women's Association (APWA), an organization which was dedicated to the welfare of the women of the country. With its headquarters in Karachi, APWA soon established centres in all the major cities of Pakistan. In due course, thanks to the efforts and stature of its President, it received international recognition through its affiliation with the United Nations.

Starting with rehabilitation of women refugees, APWA's activities rapidly extended into establishing girl's schools, women's hospitals, family planning centres, women's legal aid services, handicraft production and sales facilities, and all the other multifarious activities associated with women's welfare. Branches were established all over Pakistan, and APWA soon became an institution and a household name. Begum Liaquat Ali Khan not only devoted her efforts, energy, and formidable personality and reputation to the organization, but displayed few compunctions in wielding her husband's name and office in order to get things done for APWA. Such creativity was necessary in Pakistan, especially during the early days when, within the bureaucracy, the scramble for scarce resources was obviously intense. Furthermore, Begum Liaquat's international reputation ('a dynamo in silk', as one admiring American columnist described her) also provided considerable foreign recognition and resources to the causes that APWA pursued. My wife Diana became a member of APWA at its inception, and her active participation led to an association with Begum Liaquat, which in due course turned into a close and lifelong family friendship. It was under these circumstances that Diana and I came to know Liaquat Ali Khan, attended many of his formal and informal parties, and were privileged to have comparatively easy access to the Prime Minister's residence. I recall that in those days, the gates of 10 Victoria Road were shut only at night and a handful of policemen would be on guard duty.

2

Quaid-e-Millat Liaquat Ali Khan: 1947–1951

In der Beschränkung zeigt sich erst der Meister
(In the limitations the master shows his mastery)

Goethe

INDOMITABLE LIEUTENANT AND MARTYR

My association with Prime Minister Liaquat Ali Khan was entirely social and personal. The closest that we came to an official relationship was in the summer of 1950, when he kindly suggested that I join the Pakistan Foreign Service, saying 'I think that you and Diana will be very successful'. It was a very tempting offer, but I was unable to avail of it as I was committed to a family business which I had just joined. Nevertheless, in the course of time, thanks to the warm-hearted hospitality of Liaquat Ali Khan and Begum Ra'ana Liaquat, Diana and I became frequent visitors to 10 Victoria Road, and eventually got to know the family well. Their family comprised of their two delightful (and agreeably unspoiled) boys, Ashraf and Akbar, and Kay Miles, a friend of Ra'ana's who had become an integral part of the family. Kay, known as Billy, was devoted to Begum Ra'ana. She was her companion, adviser, secretary, speechwriter, governess to the boys, and a loving caretaker. She continued living with the family after the death of Liaquat Ali Khan until her own sad death many years later.

Following the tragic assassination of Liaquat Ali Khan in 1951, our friendship with Begum Ra'ana deepened. We exchanged visits at our respective embassies when Begum Ra'ana and I became ambassadors and at each other's homes when we were in Karachi. It grew into a lifelong association of love and affection, during the course of which I learned a great deal about Begum Ra'ana's early life: of her work with Liaquat Ali Khan; of Liaquat's work with Muhammad Ali Jinnah when they were striving for the creation of Pakistan, which was a veritable combination of dreams, struggles, and disappointments, of political friendships made, broken, and sometimes remade, and the excitement of carrying the exhilarating message of the idea of Pakistan across to the masses all over India.

By the time I got to know Liaquat, he clearly appeared to be in control of the affairs of state and his leadership seemed to have been accepted and acknowledged by politicians and populace alike. He retained his official residence at 10 Victoria Road, whilst the amiable and respectable Khwaja Nazimuddin moved into the President's House and carried out his ceremonial obligations as prescribed under the Constitution. I was later told by Liaquat that there had been a suggestion (Liaquat did not name the obsequious courtier) that, as Prime Minister, he should be provided with a Military Secretary and an ADC. The proposal was immediately shot down by the PM himself, who felt that he was a political personality and a public figure and thus should be accessible to people. These ceremonial perquisites were not for individuals but were symbols of the dignity of the high offices of presidents and governors. This admirable tradition was continued by all the distinguished successor Presidents and Prime Ministers for many years.

The tradition was subsequently demolished by Zulfikar Ali Bhutto in one of his numerous fits of megalomania, when he changed roles from President to Prime Minister. He decided to take his Military Secretary and battalion of ADCs with him to his new office, ensuring that pomp stayed with power. Nawabzada Liaquat Ali Khan, whose descent and background were steeped in nobility, carried them in his person, and had no need of extraneous trappings. He worked effectively enough through his Political Secretary, the efficient and devoted Nawab Siddique Ali Khan.

Another of the many instances in which I observed the punctilious fashion in which the leaders of Pakistan during those early years displayed their respect for the institutions of the state was at a dinner hosted by the Prime Minister in honour of Eugene Black, President of the World Bank. Before dinner, the guests were standing in small scattered groups having their cocktails, and the Prime Minister, in his usual hospitable manner, was mingling with them, exchanging pleasantries, as befits a civilized dinner. During the course of his chat with our small group, Liaquat casually mentioned that he had invited the Chief Justice to the dinner, but the latter had declined the invitation on the grounds that it was not befitting for the Chief Justice to accept an invitation from the Chief Executive for an official dinner. (Normal protocol would, of course, have rendered it entirely appropriate for the Chief Justice to have accepted an invitation from the Governor General.) Liaquat's appreciative comment was, 'it was my duty to invite him and it was perfectly correct on his part to decline it.' This small episode reflects the rectitude that characterized the holders of high office in the early days of Pakistan. The same spirit permeated the senior bureaucracy to the lower executive levels of administration. Despite all the difficulties and setbacks that afflicted the newly created state, the realization of the importance of the sanctity of institutions was both paramount and pervasive. These admirable compulsions were the essential components of the rule of law. When and why did we lose them?

Unlike the stern Jinnah (he had to be that), Liaquat Ali Khan was friendly and affable, with the grace and dignity of the born nobleman. His self-assurance derived from a combination of his birth and his achievements. Following a distinguished career at Oxford, he was called to the Bar in 1922, and entered politics immediately upon his return to India. He joined the Muslim League in 1923, becoming a Member of the UP Provincial Assembly and then of the Central Assembly. He secured recognition in both chambers for his debating skills as well as for his talent for legislative organization. These abilities, coupled with Liaquat's presence in Delhi, where he devoted his time, talent, and energy (not to mention his personal financial resources) to the Muslim League, led Jinnah to propose

Liaquat Ali Khan as General Secretary of the Muslim League in 1943. Jinnah called Liaquat 'my right hand man', a sobriquet that stuck to Liaquat for the rest of his life. 'Though a Nawabzada', Jinnah added in a prescient assessment of Liaquat, 'he was a thorough proletarian'. In my all too brief and modest association with Liaquat, I had the opportunity to observe both these aspects of his persona.

Liaquat had a benign and kindly disposition, was not easily ruffled or irritated, and had a mischievous sense of humour. At informal dinner parties at his house, he displayed his considerable skills on the *tabla* and also beat a hot drum. These gatherings, which included sing-songs, were organized by Begum Ra'ana, partly because she was an instinctive hostess and loved entertaining her friends, but mostly because she wanted to provide her husband with an opportunity to relax and spend a few hours free from the cares of state. Invitations were issued on an informal basis, often on the telephone, and the guests could almost come and go as they pleased.

Liaquat Ali Khan and Begum Ra'ana were deeply devoted to each other and to their children. This devotion is illustrated in a photograph in a truly delightful and unmistakable manner. It was taken on the lawns of 10 Victoria Road, when the Press Information Department had arranged for some well-known foreign photographer for a session at the Prime Minister's House, and allocated to him as escort a junior photographer from the department. While the foreign photographer was fussing around his subjects trying to arrange the right pose, the young Pakistani photographer took the charming picture. This was the photograph that was selected by the couple and subsequently presented to their friends.

Liaquat Ali Khan always maintained his calm and never seemed overburdened by the affairs of the state. On the contrary, he appeared to relish the challenges, both, of building a new nation and those imposed by the limitation of resources that Pakistan faced during its early existence. In the corridors of the National Assembly, he exuded the same aura of self-assured goodwill as he did in the drawing room of his residence, but once he was on the rostrum he was an altogether different person, radiating the authority of the Prime Minister and exhibiting the parliamentary skills for which he was justly famous. His third persona was his brilliance as a public speaker, and his ability to sway the people with his oratory. He achieved this in the days before rent-a-crowd or harness-a-crowd, when people went of their own volition to the *maidaan* (grounds) in thousands just to hear oratory.

Only once did I see Liaquat display his anger. We were at a small family lunch at his house. The table had been laid and cocktails served. In those days, the favourite was an old colonial concoction: chilled gin with a dash of lime juice called a gimlet. Liaquat, who was normally punctual and cheerful on such occasions, was unusually delayed and in a perceptibly bad humour. He told us that he had just had a very unpleasant episode in his office. It related to an incident connected to the Evacuee Property Law under which Muslim refugees who lost properties in India could claim compensation from properties abandoned by Hindus in Pakistan. This law, equitable in concept, was of course subject to much corruption, and was a sensitive political issue. It seems that some sycophantic bureaucrats had prepared a claim form for Liaquat, based on his considerable assets in India, allotting him an equally considerable compensation in Pakistan. Assuring him that the valuation of the assets had been entirely equitable, they submitted the file for the Prime Minister's signature. Liaquat's furious response was to throw the file across the room. He told the officials to pay an immediate visit to the *bastis* (shanty towns) in Malir and under the Queen's Road bridge. The file could be resubmitted to him after they had resettled the last of these suffering homeless refugees. Liaquat's concluding comment was 'bureaucrats of this kind will ruin us all'. Liaquat Ali Khan's indignation could not have been more righteous. In his profound and absolute love for Pakistan, he had abandoned vast agricultural lands in Karnal and many urban properties elsewhere in India. Above all, he gifted to the Government of Pakistan his splendid New Delhi residence, Gul-e-Ra'ana, on Hardinge Road, for use as Pakistan's High Commission in India. It may be mentioned here that, before leaving for Pakistan, Mr Jinnah sold his equally splendid bungalow on Aurangzeb Road to Ramkrishna Dalmia, the Marwari multimillionaire. Born and bred in the luxury of ancestral nobility, Liaquat died a virtual pauper.

On that last fateful day, Diana and I were having our evening tea in our garden when one of our domestic staff rushed to us. He gushed that he had heard on the radio that the Prime Minister had been shot whilst addressing a public meeting in Rawalpindi. We immediately left for 10 Victoria Road, where we found a large, anxious, and mostly silent crowd gathered at the gate. Ra'ana had shut herself in her room, devastated and grief stricken, but Billy told us what had happened. They too were taking tea in the garden when Chaudhry Muhammad Ali, the Secretary General, and probably the ablest civil servant in the subcontinent, came to the Prime Minister's House. On seeing him, Ra'ana was a little annoyed and told him that he was constantly 'bothering' them when the Prime Minister was in residence; why could he not leave them in peace now that he was away in Rawalpindi? At this, Muhammad Ali broke down, and weeping profusely, he said to them, 'I wish to God that I did not have to come for this.' He then broke the bitter news of Liaquat Ali Khan's assassination.

In due course, we heard the details of Liaquat's last tragic moments: of how he was felled by two bullets, and as Nawab Siddique Ali Khan went to help him, Liaquat recited the Holy Kalima, said that he had been shot ('*goli lag gayi hai*'), and recited the Holy Kalima again. Solicitous till the end about his country, Liaquat's last words were, 'God protect Pakistan'. Some days later, as a few sad friends collected with Ra'ana in her drawing room, she pulled out a book, and said to me, her eyes brimming with tears, 'Look what Liaquat was reading on his trip to Rawalpindi'. It was Arthur Koestler's *The God that Failed*.

Not much was known about Liaquat's assailant apart from his name, Said Akbar. He was killed by the police guard immediately after he fired the shots. This senseless act compounded a disastrous security failure, and immediately triggered the usual series of conspiracy theories, followed by the usual official enquiries, including one by Scotland Yard. I remember spending a great deal of time with Ra'ana on consolation visits and advising her to disregard the flurry of rumour and speculation that prevailed at the time and were repeated to her by her numerous visitors. The death of a senior Pakistani investigating police officer in a mysterious air crash, in which several documents of Liaquat's case also perished, added considerably to the uncertainty and disquiet that prevailed at the time. To date, the mystery of Liaquat's death remains unsolved.

In a Cabinet Meeting held after Liaquat Ali Khan's assassination, Begum Liaquat was awarded a pension, a P.A., a car and driver, and a ministerial residence in Bath Island, Karachi. My wife Diana and myself were among the small group of friends who helped Ra'ana to wind up her affairs at 10 Victoria Road and move to Bath Island. It was a sad and wrenching affair. To the shock of Liaquat's sudden absence was added the pitiful nature of his material legacy. His personal possessions, to the best of my recollection, consisted of his clothes, a collection of books, and a cabinet filled with cigarette lighters which he would collect as a hobby. The balance in his bank account was a little over forty-seven thousand rupees. On the other hand, on the unwritten credit column in the balance sheet was his legacy to his countrymen—Pakistan.

Since I never had the privilege of working with Liaquat as Prime Minister, my impressions are based essentially on my personal relations with his family, especially Ra'ana, and on our frequent social meetings. On these occasions, if there happened to be a political crisis brewing, I recall him being cool and unruffled. This happened at the time of the start of the canal waters dispute with India, and also at the time of the so-called Rawalpindi Conspiracy. The first crisis was not one that figured very much in the press, but it was one whose long-term implications, in human as well as political terms, could have been quite disastrous. I followed, in respectful silence, some of the discussions that Liaquat held at his residence with his ministers and officials, and noted his style of pragmatic and unruffled leadership. As the lower riparian state, we were at a clear disadvantage, a position that was further exacerbated by the prevailing political environment, with India in a state of one of its recurrent hostile attitudes. Liaquat very skilfully guided the issue into the arbitration which eventually led, after long and tortuous negotiations that continued well after his death, to the World Bank sponsored Indus Basin Treaty. The Rawalpindi Conspiracy Case was a far more emotive issue, and one that caused shock, surprise, and concern. Apart from being Prime Minister, Liaquat also held the portfolio of Defence Minister, with Iskander Mirza as Defence Secretary, but a complication was that the three Military Service Chiefs were all British. I knew nothing about the consultations that were taking place, but could not fail to notice the tension that prevailed in the atmosphere at that time at 10 Victoria Road. Equally apparent was the cool and composed demeanour of the Prime Minister as he confidently dealt with the crisis.

Although we had the occasional casual political discussion, it was only once that Liaquat sought my view on a substantial issue. He asked me whether, as a businessman, I thought that Pakistan should follow India and devalue its currency in order to remain competitive. It was at the time of the Korean War, and our cotton exports were booming. So I advised against it and he agreed and told me that the decision had been taken, and the rate stayed at nine rupees to the Sterling Pound.

Not unlike Jinnah, most of Liaquat's work for Pakistan was done before the creation of the country. A malign fate conspired to remove both leaders before either could build the institutions that would provide a stable, democratic structure to the state that Jinnah created and for which Liaquat toiled. Death stalked the tenure of Liaquat Ali Khan: a not unexpected demise brought him to office, and shortly thereafter, a totally unforeseen, cruel assassination resulted in his untimely removal. He achieved much during the comparatively short period that he served as Prime Minister, but there were disappointments and failures in a number of other aspects. His major achievement was to hold Pakistan together and strengthen the newly created government offices and administrative institutions as they came under strain from adverse political circumstances and a crippling lack of resources. He did this through the sheer force of his personality, on his integrity, probity, and on the strength of his role in the creation of Pakistan. He had truly achieved so much from so little.

Perhaps one of Liaquat's most significant decisions, and one that has been the subject of fierce debate over the years, was his acceptance of Washington's invitation for an official visit to the United States. There is a widely held belief that Liaquat had received invitations from both the United States and the Soviet Union, and that he chose to accept the former. Many years later, when I was Ambassador in Moscow, I checked the records both in Islamabad and at my post, but could find neither an invitation nor any notes or reference to this assertion. Be that as it may, Liaquat, accompanied by Begum Ra'ana, who created a sensation in her own right, and a small delegation (four or five persons, how times have changed!), had a most successful visit to the United States. Diana and I were among the group of about thirty friends who saw them off, and received them on return, at the rotunda of the old Karachi airport. The immediate impact of Liaquat's tour of the USA was a strengthening of Pakistan's military and economic resources, which were then in very dire straits. I knew at the time that the visit was an important one, but had no realization that it was the beginning of a relationship that would become one of the most complicated and tortuous in contemporary international diplomacy.

Perhaps Liaquat's greatest failure was the delay in framing a constitution. In India, Nehru had completed the task by 1950 and held the first of many free elections in 1951. Liaquat's critics have felt that the delay was deliberate, and attributed this to two factors: the first of these was the East Pakistan population majority, which could have brought in Huseyn Shaheed Suhrawardy as Prime Minister. This antipathy towards the Bengalis by the West Pakistani political elite, especially in the Punjab, manifested itself very early in the body politic of Pakistan, and eventually grew into explosive proportions, as the historical record has shown. The second criticism of Liaquat was that, though personally still popular, he had left his constituency in India, had no political grassroots in Pakistan, and needed time to create one, particularly in the heartland of the Punjab, a territory already filling with tigers on the prowl. Another charge against Liaquat was that he moved the 'Objectives Resolution', which declared Pakistan to be an 'Islamic State'. This was arguably not what Jinnah had intended. Worse still, it was construed as an instrument that provided an entry to the mullahs into the politics of the country. Liaquat himself was essentially an enlightened and moderate person. He was by no means a fundamentalist. It was just possible that he thought that by the use of this device he could both get the political support of religious leaders and also control their excesses. But this is pure speculation. History will only record that he moved the Objectives Resolution and set in train the long-term consequences that flowed from it. An immediate deleterious effect was, of course, that it compounded the delay in the framing of the Constitution.

Notwithstanding these reservations, there can be no doubt whatsoever about the greatness of Liaquat Ali Khan as a man, and of his role in the creation of Pakistan. To this day, the most common reaction of Pakistanis, even of those who never knew him or lived during his tenure, is the expression, 'If only Liaquat had lived longer'. This in itself is an epitaph as moving and as befitting as any.

The other is the title of Quaid-e-Millat bestowed upon Liaquat Ali Khan on his death by a grateful and grieving nation.

For the mystery of man's being is not only in living, but what one lives for.

Fyodor Dostoevsky

3

Years of Liberty and Public Cheer: 1951–1958

CAPRICIOUS GOVERNMENTS AND RAMBUNCTIOUS POLITICS

As I left the burial mound after Liaquat's funeral along with thousands of tearful mourners, I shared the sadness hanging over the crowd as it slowly wended its way through the choking dust-laden atmosphere. Fate, in some malign, vengeful mood, had struck a second devastating blow to the country. In what could, in the historic context, be regarded as the merest fraction of time, Pakistan lost its founder and its builder. It seemed to me that an epic era, which we had welcomed with so much enthusiasm, had come to an abrupt end. Who were going to be our leaders now, and more importantly, would they have the capacity and capability to lead the country? These same thoughts had occurred when Jinnah died, but at that time, there had been the reassuring presence of Liaquat.

Who now?

Early apprehensions had been assuaged by a prompt meeting of the Cabinet which, by a somewhat unusual measure, decided to appoint Governor General Khwaja Nazimuddin as

Prime Minister, while Ghulam Mohammad was appointed
Governor General. This decision, at the time, seemed like a
reassurance of the smoothness of the transfer of power, but
the consequences of the action would eventually reverberate
in the fortunes of the country and of Nazimuddin and
Ghulam Mohammad. Even so, for the next fifteen years
there was in Pakistan an air of unrestricted, explosive
political freedom such as has never existed since. There
was a sense of liberty that pervaded the land. The whiff of
oxygen that had come from independence from colonial
rule was still very much in the body politic of Pakistan
and its people. There was a spirit of cheerful optimism:
the government machinery had been set in place and was
functioning; industries were being set up, creating jobs as
well as products.

Of course, Liaquat Ali Khan's sudden absence left a great
vacuum amongst the political elite of the country, but the
people of Pakistan, in their usual resilient manner, went on
with their lives.

The most vivid example of this dynamic leap in socio-
economic development was manifest in the growth of
Karachi. Having absorbed the shocks of the initial post-
Partition refugee influx and the chaos rendered by it, the
city rapidly grew into one of the world's more agreeable
capitals. Its multi-ethnic Pakistani population, consisting
of Sindhis, Bengalis, Punjabis, Pathans, and Balochs lived
in harmony with emigrants from India, from Delhi, UP,
Bihar, Hyderabad, Madras, and other cities. Added to this
was the inflow of foreigners from all over the world, as

they filled the staff requirements of embassies, international organizations, and multilateral corporations eager to do business in a promising new country. Furthermore, the geographic location of Karachi, which in pre-Partition days was the entrance and take-off point for all aerial traffic into India,* continued to enjoy this status, and for many years served as a hub for most international airlines. The freedom with which people of all classes and nationalities mingled in Karachi, the exchange of ideas and cultures, the flourishing shops, hotels, clubs, cinemas, and cafes, of concerts and cabarets, had made the city into a lively and cosmopolitan metropolis.

Since Karachi was the capital of Pakistan, the Parliament and Central Government offices were also located in the city, and became an important element in the dispensation, creating opportunities for direct interaction between legislators, bureaucrats, businessmen, academics, artists, and the general public. To us, the residents of the city, it appeared as though all this had turned Karachi into a lodestar around which the rest of Pakistan revolved. Lahore, notwithstanding its urban dignity, its universities, schools, markets, bazaars, monuments, and long historical association, lost its importance, and regained its significance many years later. As for Dacca (Dhaka), it remained distant, even at that time. In the early days, flights between East

---

* The Star Gate monument (designating the 'Star of India'), which still stands at the entrance to the old International Airport, was built to commemorate the aerial entrance into India. The origin of this remnant of colonial British Indian symbolism remains unknown to most present-day residents of Karachi.

and West Pakistan involved stops or changes in Delhi or Calcutta. And, of course, the GHQ remained sullen, isolated and ominously sulking in distant and dry Rawalpindi.

To reiterate, Pakistan in the 1950s resembled an ocean liner pulsating with happy passengers, a reasonably competent ship's crew in the form of the Civil Service, but with a group of officers squabbling about the direction in which to steer the vessel, adrift in the high seas. The country lacked a clearly charted course by way of a Constitution. Each navigator had his own idea of the best compass course to follow. For some of us, who lived through those carefree days, the formation and dissolution of governments was not a matter of major concern, since all parliamentary norms and procedures were being followed. Although the country lacked a definitive Constitution, the process of government was conducted in accordance with accepted legislative practice. Moreover, the independence of the judiciary was very manifest, as were a free press and the freedom of expression and public discussion. There was a veritable cultural explosion throughout the country, with artists, musicians, poets, and dramatists flourishing all over the place, filling it with a burst of creative activity.

And then there was Abdul Hafeez Kardar and his band of merry cavaliers, who took Pakistan cricket from obscurity onto the world's highest echelons. My interactions with the political leaders of the time were almost entirely social and personal, a consequence of the easy informality that prevailed during that period. Amongst them were Iskander Mirza, Huseyn Shaheed Suhrawardy, and a number of

other politicians, including Mujibur Rahman from Bengal,
Mian Iftikharuddin from the Punjab, the Haroon brothers,
Yusuf and Mahmood, from Sindh, and Qazi Isa from
Balochistan.

A vivid example of the freedom that characterized those
days was an informal association of my friends who
would meet every Friday evening at Air Cottage, a tiny
residence occupied by Sattu Kureishi (Squadron Leader
Safdar Kureishi M.B.E., RAF) and his brothers Enver
(Abu) and Omar (Omo), incongruously situated right
next to the huge airship hanger (later commonly known
as *kaala chapra*). It had been built by the British for the
ill-fated R101 airship that crashed in Belgium on its
maiden flight, leaving this enormous structure as a Karachi
landmark for over half a century. Sattu was an aeronautical
engineer with a distinguished war record; Abu was an
erudite officer in the Press Information Department;
and Omo was a superb journalist, editor, and a cricket
commentator (I was his companion). They belonged to
a large family whose members collectively possessed the
most extraordinary wit, intelligence, and versatile talent.
The Friday evening sessions that began with the getting
together of a few friends soon became an institution in the
Karachi of the 1950s, attracting the widest and most diverse
attendance. These included cabinet ministers, politicians,
civil servants, diplomats from the embassies located in
Karachi, journalists, writers, artists, poets, businessmen
and sportsmen. Aziz Ahmed, G. Ahmed, Huseyn Shaheed
Suhrawardy, Zulfikar Ali Bhutto, J. A. Rahim, Mujibur

Rahman, Mian Iftikharuddin, Arnold Toynbee, Stephen Spender, Qurratulain Hyder (Annie), Andre Kozlov from the Soviet Embassy (we all knew he was KGB), and Alan Wolf from the US Embassy (we all knew he was CIA) were among those who would come. Of course there was a host of hardy perennial regulars, such as myself, Bobby Faruki, Yunus M. Saeed, and Afzal Khan. Discussions were as stimulating and freewheeling as could be expected from such a lavish intellectual collection. At one of the sessions at Air Cottage, I overheard a heated discussion between Suhrawardy and Mujibur Rahman, when the latter berated his leader for accepting the concept of parity between East and West Pakistan despite the Bengalis being in the majority. Suhrawardy urged Mujib to be 'realistic'. Insistence on majority rule 'would mean the break up of Pakistan, and I have no intention of doing that', retorted Suhrawardy—a supremely patriotic sentiment and an ominously prophetic thought.

HUSEYN SHAHEED SUHRAWARDY

My personal association with Huseyn Shaheed Suhrawardy was by no means close, but I got to admire and like him tremendously. A short, tubby man, with highly intelligent piercing eyes and a sardonic expression on his face, he had an altogether puckish appearance, with a matching sense of humour. He was an extremely erudite man, with a mind fine-honed by his forensic legal skills. The fun-loving Suhrawardy liked the company of pretty women—I frequently saw him at nightclubs such as 'Le Gourmet', dancing late into the night. Yet on the next morning, his mind was as clear and razor-sharp as ever. I know this from personal experience, since Suhrawardy, when not in office, was a legal counsel for my business corporation.

In our personal conversations, we almost never discussed Pakistan's politics, and spent more time discussing art and music. Not surprisingly, I found him to be a deep humanist, profoundly empathetic towards the deprived and the oppressed. In his biography, his cousin Shaista Suhrawardy Ikramullah writes of Suhrawardy's first speech in the Constituent Assembly of Pakistan:

> His speech was motivated by consideration for fundamental human values which transcended parochial considerations … 'open your minds and hearts and take within your fold the non-Muslim minority'.

Apart from this fervent streak of humanism that characterized his policies, Suhrawardy had, in my view, two accomplishments that were of fundamental importance to the state of Pakistan. The first was that he was, along with Fazlul Haq and Khwaja Nazimuddin, one of the three leaders who brought Bengal into Pakistan. The second, just as important, was the establishment of friendly relations between Pakistan and the Peoples Republic of China. This visionary act of diplomacy was conducted almost as soon as he had assumed the office of Prime Minister in 1956, against strong United States pressure and at a time when China had almost no friends outside of the communist bloc. Suhrawardy took a large Pakistani delegation to

Peking (Beijing) in 1956, and Zhou En-lai responded with an equally effusive visit to Pakistan in 1967. Subsequent Pakistani leaders, notably Zulfikar Ali Bhutto, have asserted their authorship to Pakistan-China friendship, but it was Suhrawardy who had the acumen, vision, and foresight to fathom the importance and depth of this relationship, and to establish diplomatic ties that have been the cornerstone of Pakistan's foreign policy in the decades that followed. It remains so to date. After Ayub Khan took over as President (in 1958), Suhrawardy was indicted in the EBDO (Elective Bodies Disqualification Ordinance) controversy. I followed with interest and admiration the spirited and incisive legal defence that he himself conducted in court. He was convicted and imprisoned for a while and left for Europe after his release. Alone and sorrowful, he died of a heart attack in a hotel room in Beirut. A vast crowd gathered at his funeral in Dacca, where I was also present. The love that people felt for Suhrawardy was palpable at his funeral.

Huseyn Shaheed Suhrawardy was brilliant, erudite, compassionate, and fun-loving. I was sorry that my only formal contact with him was to seek legal advice and guidance. Diplomacy under his direction would have been a fascinating exercise.

Descriptions of the relaxed, tolerant atmosphere that pervaded the Pakistan of the 1950s are legion and too numerous to recount. But there is one incident, hitherto almost unknown, that is worthy of record simply as an illustration of the relations that once prevailed between the rulers and the ruled. It was related to me by

Prince Miangul Aurangzeb of Swat, an old school friend of mine, and concerns his father-in-law, Ayub Khan. He had been recently nominated as Defence Minister under Iskander Mirza, after the latter's assumption to the office of Governor General of Pakistan. Ayub Khan and Iskander Mirza were good friends. One evening, Iskander invited Ayub to accompany him on a drive to Hawke's Bay. As was often the case in those days, they left the Government House in a car without a flag, escort, or any of the other vulgar trappings of power and authority. Who worried about 'security' in those days? Pakistanis were a trusting lot and were generally law-abiding citizens. On the way back, their car broke down—and since cell phones did not then exist—the vehicle's distinguished occupants were properly stranded! By good fortune, they were able to stop a taxi and asked the driver to take them to Karachi, identifying themselves to the taxi driver. The driver noticeably suspended credibility until, following his passengers' directions, they actually arrived at the Government House and were duly saluted by the guards at the gatehouse. Since neither of the distinguished occupants of the car had any money on their persons, they were obliged to borrow the cab fare from the guard commander—embarrassment shifting from the humble cab driver to the high-powered duo.

ISKANDER MIRZA

I knew Iskander Mirza since the early days of Pakistan when, as Defence Secretary, he worked closely with Liaquat

Ali Khan and was frequently at the Prime Minister's House on official as well as social occasions. Moreover, his son Humayun had been with me at the Doon School in Dehradun, and is still one of my close friends. Iskander was amongst the earliest Indians to be selected for a course at Sandhurst. He graduated as an officer in the Indian Army, and till the end of his life had the ramrod stance and bearing of a born soldier. He was also amongst the first Indian officers to be transferred from the Army to the Indian Political Service, the elite unit of the British Indian Administration. Following years of distinguished service in the North-West Frontier, Iskander Mirza was appointed Defence Secretary at the creation of Pakistan.

Competent and ambitious, Iskander Mirza followed the machinations of the politicians with an obvious combination of disapproval and contempt. Meanwhile, the 1953 anti-Ahmadi riots in Lahore had compelled the weak civilian government to impose Martial Law in the city. General Azam Khan, the Martial Law Administrator, did a stern and efficient job in restoring order, a consequence of which was a rise in the popularity of the army. The lesson was not lost on Iskander, who never hesitated to display his military connections. When conditions got difficult in East Pakistan, a weak and vacillating Prime Minister Khwaja Nazimuddin sent Iskander as Governor of the province. The move, and the direct political exposure, whetted an already voracious appetite for power. After his stint in Dacca, Iskander returned to Karachi. He was determined to make his contribution to the welfare of Pakistan or his own destiny, depending upon the point of view of the observer. He was made Member of the Cabinet, following the intrigues and infighting engineered largely by Governor General Ghulam Mohammad. On 17 April 1953, Ghulam Mohammad seized the excuse provided by the general lawlessness that followed the Ahmadi agitation and its suppression, and invoked Section 10 of the Provisional Constitution to dismiss Prime Minister Khwaja Nazimuddin. This was despite the fact that Nazimuddin had only recently proved his majority by getting the budget passed in the House, and also despite a last pathetic, quixotic attempt to retain his office by an appeal to the British High Commissioner for an intercession by the Queen on his behalf.

Ghulam Mohammad's action could well be regarded as the *first* coup in Pakistan's history. But it was achieved with a smoothness that left the country comparatively unperturbed. It was only in retrospect that I realized the import of the action taken by the Governor General. One of the subsequent consequences was that Iskander was eventually moved to a position which put him a step closer to the office of Governor General, which he duly assumed in August 1955. Shortly after, when Pakistan became a Republic in February 1956, Iskander Mirza became President, thus becoming the last Governor General of Pakistan and the first President of Pakistan.

My personal association with Iskander Mirza during this period was comparatively slight, being restricted to formal meetings at receptions and the occasional encounter through his son Humayun. Historical record shows that this was the period when Pakistan and the United States moved towards a military alliance. It also reveals the adroit diplomacy that Mirza and Ayub displayed in this process. Coincidentally, it was also the time when Iskander Mirza's son Humayun married Dody, daughter of US Ambassador Horace Hildreth. Resemblance to medieval royal matrimonial alliances linking states is of course evocative, but was in this case quite coincidental. I can testify that it was truly a romantic association.

As far as Iskander Mirza was concerned, even I, who was so far away from the corridors of power, could clearly observe his contempt for politicians as he manoeuvred amongst them, playing one against the other. Iskander operated like the political agents of bygone colonial days, rewarding one tribal malik and punishing another, except that it was now the modern state of Pakistan and not the old North-West Frontier of India.

As Governor General, Mirza, lacking a popular political base, cultivated the army along with Ayub Khan, whose admission into the Cabinet as Defence Minister formalized his position and increased his power and access in the political life of Pakistan. As a friend (he was an occasional visitor at our home and played bridge with my wife Diana), and also through my close association with his son Humayun, I followed Iskander's activities with interest. I was obviously very happy when he became Governor General. Naturally, I remained completely unaware of his workings in the political field, both domestic and international, but I did notice his growing friendship with

Zulfikar Ali Bhutto, a bright young barrister who had recently returned to Pakistan and joined the chambers of our family's legal adviser, Dingomal Narainsingh. It was obvious that Iskander had not only recognized a bright and dynamic young talent, but was also determined to groom him. He accordingly made Bhutto a Member of the Pakistan delegation to the United Nations General Assembly Meeting in New York, and to the Law of the Sea Conference in Geneva (from where Bhutto addressed an obsequious letter to Mirza describing him as a greater leader than Jinnah).

On 7 October 1958, President Iskander Mirza abrogated the Constitution of Pakistan and declared Martial Law. He inducted Zulfikar Ali Bhutto into the Cabinet and was assigned the post of Commerce Minister. The incandescent Shooting Star was low on the horizon at that time, but had indubitably entered the firmament. Ayub Khan was designated as Chief Martial Law Administrator, with the three Armed Services Chiefs (Air Marshal Asghar Khan, General Muhammad Musa Khan, and Admiral A. R. Khan), and Aziz Ahmed as Deputy Chief Martial Law Administrator. This seizure of power by means of a Martial Law Declaration was, in my view, *the* cardinal sin in the political life of Pakistan, and one from which the country has never recovered.

It soon became evident that there could be no coexistence between Iskander and Ayub (two lions cannot live together in the same cage). Only a few weeks into the declaration of Martial Law, on 27 October 1958, Iskander Mirza was removed from power by Ayub Khan in a peaceful but dramatic fashion and exiled to London. The next year, I called on him and his wife Nahid at their small flat off Exhibition Road, where they were obviously living in what could best be described as modest circumstances. In our conversation, it was clear to me that whereas Iskander was pragmatic enough to accept the slings and misfortunes of politics, he was deeply hurt by the behaviour of so many whom he had thought were his friends 'and now run a mile if they see me in Piccadilly'. He told me that he was living on his two pensions: one that he was getting from his Indian Political Service and the other as President of Pakistan. His income was being supplemented by remittances from his son Humayun. There was also a sneering rumour that he was made a Director at Veeraswamy's, a well known Indian Restaurant on Regent Street. This is irrefutable evidence that, in stark contrast to many of his successor rulers of Pakistan, Iskander Mirza was honest and scrupulous. *Sic transit gloria mundi* (Thus passes the glory of the world).

Ayub Khan's assumption to power as President of Pakistan in 1958, though not entirely unexpected at the time, was the second thunderbolt after Iskander Mirza's Martial Law Declaration. A bewildered and somewhat nervous nation sat glued to the radio awaiting announcements and news of developments. These came in a series of stern edicts classified by Martial Law Numbers, many of them specifying death by hanging for infringement. I remember my brothers Khursheed, Minoo, and myself seated on my lawn, listening to Ayub's speech on the radio with a mixture of anticipation and trepidation. When Ayub came to the bit where he said, 'the honest businessman has nothing to fear', my brother Khursheed's sardonic murmur was 'too true—he went out of business years ago'. And when Ayub concluded his speech, by justifying his reasons for taking over the reins of power, and his future course of action (the rhetoric of all successor military rulers), my brother Minoo, ever the historian, murmured, 'This is the end of "Merrie Pakistan", now we have Cromwell'.

4

Field Marshal Mohammad
Ayub Khan: 1958–1969

*Next to knowing when to seize an opportunity,
the most important thing in life is to know when
to forego an advantage.*

Benjamin Disraeli

*__Military Dictatorship:__ Time of benevolent despotism, dignity,
bearing, and probity in office, nationwide political stability,
attended by the most substantial economic development in the
history of Pakistan, and also perhaps a period of the soundest
public administration, followed by a compulsive, desperate, but
futile quest for popular political legitimacy, and a turbulent
return to Military Dictatorship.*

The thunderbolt of Ayub Khan's takeover reverberated all
over Pakistan. Ironically, the exceptions remained the rural
and the urban proletariats. Though they constitute the
vast majority of the country, they have always remained
unmoved by the games played by politicians. For them, in
the poignant words of W. B. Yeats, 'no likely end will bring
them loss or leave them happier than before'.

Initially, Ayub kept the upper echelons of his administration
(Ministers, Governors, DCMLAs) more or less intact. But

he introduced Martial Law Courts, and sent further shock waves through the affluent citizenry by dismissing a number of senior civil servants and arresting some prominent businessmen. However, to the best of my recollection, this khaki dominance was comparatively short-lived. Troops were back in their barracks in a matter of months, military courts were disbanded without having imposed too many harsh sentences, and a military-bureaucratic nexus slowly but perceptibly began to take shape. In due course, this would be joined by a third element, the entrepreneurs (industrial and commercial), whose inclusion completed the composition and establishment of the decade-long Ayub era. It was a solid West Pakistan structure, with a thinly disguised East Pakistan facade, which began to crumble no sooner than it was plastered on.

The early decision by the Martial Law administration to establish Islamabad as the capital of Pakistan, and the brusque nature in which it was built and occupied, was a political act of breathtaking proportions. Karachi had become a de facto capital through an evolution of circumstances following Partition, and had acquired a cosmopolitan and multi-ethnic entity that was representative of the entire country. By contrast, nobody could fail to notice that the proposed new capital, Islamabad, had been situated even further from East Pakistan than Karachi, and that it had been located as a suburb of Rawalpindi and the GHQ (General Headquarters). To continue the architectural metaphor, Ayub Khan's hammer blows not only scraped off the facade, but went on to construct a new edifice in a relocated, distant environment. The signal to the people in distant Bengal could not have been more clear or more ominous. Prime Minister Khwaja Nazimuddin, one of the most distinguished and respected Muslim League Bengali politicians, had just secured a majority in the National Assembly, having passed the Budget, but this was of no consequence. He had nevertheless been summarily relegated to his ancestral home in Dacca (Dhaka). Power now lay not with the people but with the gun. The resentment that this evoked in East Pakistan became vividly evident to me in my conversations with friends, politicians, businessmen, and the laity during my visits to Dacca (Dhaka) shortly after the imposition of the 1958 Martial Law. This pattern of provocation and resentment continued to grow in deleterious fashion over the coming years, until mutually concealed feelings of confrontation inexorably moved into open political expression and, finally, to the calamitous tragedy of 1971.

However, all this was in the distant unforeseen future. When Martial Law was first imposed in Pakistan, there was a sense of submission rather than fear, but even this gradually changed. Ayub very wisely decided to send the troops back to the barracks and to resort to the civil bureaucracy for the administration of the country. He had at his disposal a superb cadre of trained, competent, and dedicated civil servants, and he utilized them wisely and well. There followed almost a decade of tranquillity and economic development which remains unmatched in the history of Pakistan. In my view, the accumulation of national wealth, and the economic momentum generated at that time still retain their presence in whatever little force drives the economy of the country in its current battered and sluggish state. The sense of order, initially created under the threatening cloud of Martial Law in 1958, gradually extended over the country. As the troops went back to their barracks and bureaucrats moved into their offices, Pakistan entered a promising period of tranquillity. This in turn provided the base for economic growth and development. A congruence between Harvard-trained Pakistani economists and foreign advisers at the Finance and Economic Affairs Ministries and the Planning Commission was witnessed, along with an emerging group of domestic and foreign entrepreneurs in Pakistan's market place. Economic development quickly moved from a gentle canter into an impressive gallop. I recall foreign investors flocking to Pakistan with capital and know-how, combining with Pakistani traders turned industrialists, in their enthusiastic praise for the Ayub administration and the wise policies that ensured a stable government combined with imaginative economic management.

From this moment, Pakistan entered what I regard, in retrospect, as a halcyon period. It lasted a couple of years less than a decade, and it was a time when, speaking as the common man that I then was, it truly felt an era of peace and prosperity. The government administration moved smoothly and efficiently, and generally enjoyed the trust and the confidence of the people. True, there was a certain amount of corruption, and occasional tales did emerge, but

they were largely marginal, especially when compared to
what occurred subsequently and exists now. The president,
governors, and senior officials were above reproach, and
were motivated by a sense of duty, free of venality. This
was my view as a businessman who had lived and worked
during that period. And I continue to maintain my
opinion. The Five Year Plan, skilfully drafted and carefully
administered in a cooperative effort between Pakistani
administrators and foreign advisers, formed the framework
for the country's impressive development. Years later, when
I had left the private sector and moved into government
and was serving as Pakistan's Ambassador in Tokyo, I had
a talk with a visiting South Korean Vice Finance Minister,
who told me that they had replicated our First Five Year
Plan. 'At that time, you were our model on what to do.
Then what happened?' He added in an impish manner, 'You
are still our model. But on what not to do!'

To return to the early Ayub development period,
industries and factories were springing up all over the
country. Agricultural production was good, thanks to
the administration's concentration on this sector by
constructing dams and fertilizer factories, so that food was
plentiful and cheap, and employment was booming. There
was a spurt in banking and finance—new banks were not
only springing up but were shifting from the old *seth* (rich
banker or merchant) domination to modern technology-
driven administration and standards. Communications met
the increasing demands of the economy, with the railways
functioning efficiently, road transport expanding, and the

shipping industry burgeoning. Above all, the Pakistan International Airlines (PIA), under the dynamic and legendary Nur Khan and skilled professionals like Enver Jamal, had become one of the world's leading airlines, so much so that it was helping to start up airlines in the United Arab Emirates, Malta, Malaysia, Singapore, and Indonesia. It was a time to boast about being a Pakistani, and never more so when one boarded a PIA aircraft at some distant, foreign airport. An air of optimism prevailed in the country, with a belief that although deficiencies undoubtedly existed, these could be overcome.

In the field of foreign affairs, we observed how Pakistan's standing invoked increasing respect, particularly for the manner in which it conducted its relations with the US, China, and the USSR, the three superpowers that dominated the world at that time. The international media, with a somewhat excess of flourish, termed Ayub Khan the 'De Gaulle of Asia'. In the world chancelleries, his dominant and impeccable appearance cut an impressive figure. A contemporary newspaper photograph showed Ayub, Zhou En-lai, Sukarno, Tito, and Nasser standing together at the Cairo airport. That photograph seemed to say it all.

But even as we floated in these clouds of comfort, many of us had our doubts and apprehensions. Disparities increased visibly between the rich and the poor, the army and the civil, and above all between East and West Pakistan. Like all military despots (even one as benevolent as Ayub), the ruler sought legitimacy, and in the process stumbled into the unfamiliar mire of participatory democracy, where results are obtained not by the barking of orders but by persuasion, arm twisting, duplicity, and compromise. Above all, ten years of Ayub's rule, comparative benevolence and economic wellbeing nonwithstanding, had led to a nationwide sense of fatigue and surfeit bordering on revulsion. I doubt that Ayub, like all of his predecessors and successors, had ever read Machiavelli. If they had, they would have concurred with the Florentine's observation in *The Prince*, that 'for it may be said of men in general that they are ungrateful, voluble, dissemblers, anxious to avoid danger and covetous of gain'.

Hitherto, my association with Ayub had been that of a citizen, observing and appreciating his political activities from a distance. Our only meetings were a formal handshake at public receptions. However, in the later stage of Ayub's rule, I found myself in the government, where my fielding position was generally at cover point.

My first one-to-one meeting with Ayub Khan took place in his office in circa October 1964, when he confirmed my appointment as High Commissioner to Ghana. The extremely favourable impression that he created upon me at the time has remained with me. The impact of his leadership was clearly evident in the Foreign Ministry when I first entered the service in mid-1965, despite the more immediate presence of heavyweights such as Foreign Minister Zulfikar Ali Bhutto and Foreign Secretary Aziz Ahmed. Ayub's power and reputation were at their crest, both at home and abroad, and although Bhutto's left incline imprint on the Foreign Office were clearly evident at the time, it seemed just as clearly evident that Ayub was intent on a course correction. My entry into diplomacy, and my interaction with Pakistan's political leadership, thus commenced during this period of latent internal rivalry.

Shortly after I assumed my post as High Commissioner to Ghana, there occurred the 1965 war with India, followed by the Tashkent Declaration. These were, of course, seminal events in terms of international relations in general, and South Asia in particular, but meant for me a change of masters in Islamabad. Ayub had completed his course correction: Bhutto and Aziz Ahmed were gone and were replaced by Sharifuddin Pirzada and S. M. Yusuf. The fact that I was friends with both the incoming and outgoing incumbents not only eased the transition for me in personal terms, but also helped in the implementation of policy directives of the changed dispensation.

During my tenure in West Africa, my only contact with President Ayub was in connection with Ghana's President Kwame Nkrumah's stopover in Karachi on his way to Peking (Beijing) and Hanoi. It was considered an official visit, despite its brief duration (about four hours), and included all the protocol and paraphernalia associated with such an occasion. I had prepared a short but intensive brief, together with talking points, for the President, which was used in his discussions with Nkrumah. It is a measure of the man's gracious qualities that when we met some months later, Ayub thanked me for my effort. Just about the moment that Ayub and the Guard of Honour had seen Nkrumah off at the Karachi airport, in Accra, the Ghanian military had inititated a coup, which was successfully completed by the time Nkrumah arrived in Peking. It was left to China's Ambassador Huang Hua, one of the world's ablest diplomats, to inform Nkrumah of the disaster that had befallen him. Nobody present at the Karachi airport ceremony could have imagined that the departure of the honoured guest would have been quite so definitive. 'Osagyefo', the first great African idol, had fallen. Nor could it have then been visualized that the same fate would extend its cruel, icy hand upon Field Marshal Ayub Khan, the 'De Gaulle of Asia'.

At the end of my tenure in Ghana, I was expecting a return to private life. But on my return to Pakistan, I was informed that I would be reassigned to Romania (with concurrent accreditation to Bulgaria), and that I was to open our mission in Bucharest in time for a forthcoming state visit by President Ayub Khan. Observing the new order that prevailed when I returned to Pakistan, I found that not only had there been a perceptible change in the concept of the direction of our foreign policy, but that there had been a physical change in the Foreign Office itself, which had shifted its location (reluctantly, if not dragged kicking and screaming, I am told), from the stately old High Court premises in Karachi to a newly constructed hotel building in Islamabad.

Following the usual briefings from the desk officers, there were the substantive meetings with Foreign Secretary S. M. Yusuf and Foreign Minister Sharifuddin Pirzada, who

informed me that he would be on the President's delegation
to Romania. I then had to call on President Ayub, which
was my second meeting with him, and it turned out to be
as pleasant as the first. He had survived the shocks of the
1965 war with India, and with Tashkent, but these had
contributed to the disaffection in the country. Bhutto and
Mujib had commenced their agitation, and it was clear that
a combination of these factors had shaken the foundation
of Ayub's domestic order. However, when I called upon
him, although he appeared to have been affected by these
adverse developments, he was nevertheless as calm and
gracious as ever. We discussed the arrangements as for his
Romanian visit (he would come from Paris, which was,
of course, the more important aspect of the trip), and I
presented him with a short brief on the political climate of
the country and its leadership, along with cautionary advice
about expectations on economic cooperation, neutrality
on political affairs, with the possibility of a compulsive
Romanian offer of mediation on Kashmir an obvious non-
starter.

On my return to Bucharest, I started working on the
President's visit at the same time as I was looking around
for a suitable embassy residence. Needless to say, this was
a complicated affair. Ayub was coming with a fairly large
delegation, although the logistics presented no difficulties
for me since those were being handled entirely by the host
government. I had to only inform them of the numbers and
ranks of the guests. President Ayub Khan and his daughter
Nasim would be accommodated in one of the palaces of

the former King, and the rest of the delegation in state guest houses and hotels, according to their rank. Transport would also be provided on the same basis. The logistics for a state visit to a communist country in those days was never a problem for the ambassador, since they were always efficiently handled by the host government. In the case of Ayub's visit to Romania, the political and economic issues also presented no problems, since the positions of both sides were well known, and it was accepted that the visit was essentially a gesture of solidarity between two countries that were following comparatively independent and neutral policies.

Being aware of Ayub Khan's fondness for *shikar* (hunting) I arranged a few shoots for him. The Romanians threw in a trip on the Danube, an excursion to the Carpathians, including a visit to Brandt Castle, the seat of the bloodthirsty Count Dracula (the symbolism puzzled Ayub a bit), and a session at the opera, from which we left at the first interval—the delegation through unfamiliarity with the medium and I because of the deplorable quality of the performance. Ayub's courteous 'I don't want to break up the party' was met with the firm reassurance that he was doing no such thing.

Ayub's discussions with the Romanian leaders, the wily and odious Ceausescu and the voluble Prime Minister Maurer, were conducted with skill and a quiet dignity. He deftly deflected their offer to mediate on Kashmir. It was clear by late 1969 that Ayub had honed his skills in international diplomacy, and it was no surprise that he turned in an impressive performance in Romania. The visit was a memorable success and ended with the usual plethora of mutual congratulations and pledges of goodwill.

Three incidents of the visit, all connected with Ayub, remain in my memory. The first concerns my request to the Romanians that the Israeli ambassador should not be invited to the arrival ceremony at the airport. The evasive answer I received was that the Foreign Office had taken note of my request. This evasion continued until I took up the matter with Prime Minister Maurer, who stated to me frankly that, in keeping with the Romanian foreign policy, an invitation would have to be issued, but the Israeli ambassador would be requested not to attend. Maurer agreed with me when I said that the ambassador would be guided by instructions received from his government and not by advice from the Romanian Foreign Office. He suggested the 'De Gaulle solution', whereby, the visiting dignitary walked down the line of ambassadors and gave them a general greeting of 'Good Morning, Your Excellencies!' This fatuous issue of protocol generated a series of cipher telegrams between the Foreign Office and myself. As it turned out, the Israeli ambassador never showed up at the airport, and Ayub told me later, with a chuckle, 'if anyone is kind and courteous enough to come to the airport and greet me, then I would certainly shake his hand.'

The next anecdote relates to an informal conversation we had when Ayub was relaxing in the garden of the Romanian palace. He recounted an event at a Karachi hotel a few weeks earlier, where he was chief guest at a dinner given by the Zoroastrian Association in commemoration of the birthday of Prophet Zarathustra. In his welcome speech, the President of the Zoroastrian Association threw in three requests. The first was that Indian Parsi girls who marry Pakistani boys should get Pakistani passports immediately. Ayub told me that he 'thought it a reasonable request'. The next was for import license for sandalwood used in the Parsi Fire Temples. Ayub thought this too to be 'a legitimate request'. The third request was for an increase in the number of visas to priests from India in order to make up for the shortage of Parsi priests in Pakistan. At this, Ayub's eyes twinkled mischievously, and with a broad grin he said to me, 'I said to myself, *o bewakoofon, you don't know how lucky you are: hum innko door rakhna chahtey hain, aur tum innko laana chahtey ho!*' (Oh you fools. You don't know how lucky you are! We are trying to get rid of them, and you want to bring more!)

The third incident occurred when, at the end of the visit, Ayub chaired a wind-up session, attended by eight or ten senior members of the delegation. He dictated to the cipher assistant a telegram for M. M. Ahmed, Chairman of our Planning Commission, outlining our discussions with the Romanian authorities and the conclusions reached. After he had finished, he looked up at us and said, 'I think that about covers it, don't you?' Everyone was in laudatory agreement, but I thought that Ayub had overlooked one important issue and said so. Whereupon the courtiers jumped on me, claiming loudly that the telegram was fine. It had been 'dictated by the President himself' and how dare anyone suggest changes, etc. etc. Ayub allowed the storm to subside, then deliberately turning to the assistant said, 'Add this', and dictated the amendment. Looking directly at me he asked, 'Does this meet your suggestion, ambassador?' But the courtiers had the last word and chorused, 'now the telegram becomes even more clear!' As we dispersed from the meeting, I thought to myself that the man had lived in this sea of sycophancy for nearly ten years—surviving with an intact level head would require superhuman qualities.

After Ayub's return home from his trip to France and Romania, Pakistan was host to a number of important foreign visitors, including Soviet Prime Minister Kosygin. But the political structure created by Ayub Khan had begun to unravel. This disintegration has already been the subject of record and analysis by historians and is a process that will doubtless continue. My purpose, as already indicated, is to record the personal impressions of an observer who was marginally involved in the political events that moved Pakistan into convulsion after a placid ten years. This period of prosperity included the benefits of the Green Revolution.

In the backdrop of the political fatigue induced by the long period of one-man rule (regardless of the benign nature of the despotism), there were four elements that I perceived at the time to be responsible for Ayub Khan's downfall. The first of these was the presidential elections in Pakistan, during the course of which the formidable Miss Fatima Jinnah, combining in a vigorous campaigning style her personal magnetism with the prevalent countrywide fatigue and discontent, achieved a close-run result. This was the first jolt that Ayub Khan received to his confidence since he assumed office a decade earlier. When I met him just after his re-election, Ayub looked tired and pensive; not the triumphant victor at all. Rumours about pressures and rigging during the elections were rife at the time. Were these true? And if so, was this a sign of a troubled conscience? Ayub was essentially a gentleman.

The second was the serious illness that struck Ayub in 1968. A heart attack, followed by surgery in the United States, put him out of action at a critical moment in his political career. Those were the days when cardiac treatment had not reached its current level of sophistication, and Ayub was never the same man after his return from Texas to Pakistan.

The third element was the public expression of dissatisfaction and outrage, possibly sparked by Miss Fatima Jinnah's electoral campaign that was by now aboard in the country. Although I did not have any personal meetings or contact with Ayub during these troubled times, one could see from the newly established television, and from radio shows and the press, that the President was under increasing duress. Politicians of every description came out of the woodwork, whilst the incompetent creations of Ayub's artificial system disappeared from view. Most important of all, the two *real* politicians, Zulfikar Ali Bhutto and Sheikh Mujibur Rahman, had begun to cast their charismatic spell in their chosen regions, Bhutto in West Pakistan and Mujib in East Pakistan.

Through all this, Ayub, though cognizant of the subterranean tremors which precede an earthquake, seemed unable to prevent the catastrophe itself. At one moment, as he was threshing around with the politicians and changing ministers through appointments and dismissals, one of his advisers suggested that sacking a particularly unpopular minister would restore confidence and order. Ayub's realistic response was, 'It is my head that they want—not anybody else's'.

The fourth, and in my view, perhaps the most significant factor in the toppling of the Ayub regime was the 1965 war with India, and the Tashkent Agreement that ensued. This is, of course, a matter of history and a subject for historians. Mine is a recollection of those times and a personal evaluation of the causes and consequences of that particular war and peace. I feel that its origins were in the sun-baked, salty marshlands of the Rann of Kutch, where the delta of the mighty Indus mingles with the deserts of Sindh and Kathiawar, and debouches into the Arabian Sea. As long as sovereignty over the entire territory was exercised by the British Raj, no one really knew or cared where one province began and the other ended, a benign neglect that was the dream of every cartographer. After independence, however, the dream turned into a nightmare, and defining the international border between India and Pakistan extended attention from cartographers to local administrators to provincial politicians to national politicians and finally to the military. In the meanwhile, poor fishermen from both sides, who had no idea of what was going on since they employed the most primitive aid of navigation, were brutally informed of border violations through capture and incarceration.

More serious was the escalation of the confrontation between the armed forces of India and Pakistan, which had gradually been inducted into the region, and which inevitably led to armed skirmishes. These in turn escalated into a military conflict, involving troops at the brigade level, and provoked widespread concern. International persuasion, coupled with an unaccustomed display of good sense in both Islamabad and New Delhi, led to a ceasefire, followed by agreement for arbitration under UN auspices in Geneva. In the tripartite negotiations, Pakistan was represented by an Iranian diplomat, India by a Yugoslav, and the Chairman was a Swede. I followed some of those hearings (amongst the most boring that I have ever attended), but the results were positive, and in spite of the nebulous terrain, an agreement was reached and an international border was delineated. This was a minor triumph for Pakistan's diplomacy, since India had been dragged out of a war and onto a conference table. But unfortunately, the conclusions drawn were entirely wrong, and the hawks in the Pakistan establishment (Bhutto, Aziz Ahmed, Akhtar Malik, et al.), in the disastrous belief that they could do the same thing again in Kashmir, launched 'Operation Gibraltar'. Many years later, I discussed this with Altaf Gohar, with whom I enjoyed a close and lasting friendship, and who had become one of Ayub Khan's closest confidants (including ghost writing his autobiography *Friends Not Masters*). I told Altaf that on the infrequent occasions that I had any discussions with Ayub, I was impressed by his clear determination that 'Kashmir is important to me, but not so important as Pakistan'. Then what happened? How did the hawks trap him into approving Operation Gibraltar? Altaf said that he had once put the same question to Ayub, whose answer was, 'My error was not to have established a counter syndicate'. This was Army Staff College talk for a 'syndicate' of officers to propose a plan of action and a 'counter syndicate' of officers to criticize it. And so, Ayub moved from the Rann of Kutch to Operation Gibraltar.

'Men commit the error of not knowing when to limit their hopes'. **Machiavelli**

I was Ambassador in Romania during the last tumultuous days of the Ayub administration, during which time I was called to Islamabad for consultations and informed by Foreign Secretary Yusuf that I had been posted to Moscow. This was an exciting challenge, and after a hurried farewell visit to Bucharest and Sofia, I returned to Pakistan and immersed myself in some substantive briefings. Thanks to the initiatives recently taken by President Ayub, relations with the USSR had shown a promising improvement, and there seemed to be several avenues which were worth exploring. We had no illusions about the close Indo-Soviet ties, but the previous latent hostility from Moscow had abated, and we seemed to be at a moment of slack water, with the tide at neither an ebb nor flow. But these considerations, though important, were overshadowed by the events taking place at home, where the opposition to

Ayub was increasingly widespread, and his failure to cope with it becoming correspondingly manifest.

I did not have a chance to meet Ayub during those last turbulent days, but his bitterness and bewilderment were apparent, and I was deeply troubled to see the blows that were being dealt to him by a malign fate that seemed bent on his humiliation. He was essentially a good, honest, and sincere man, a patriot who was devoted to the welfare of his country. Even his cardinal sin of declaring Martial Law was mitigated, in my view, by the association of others in the action—Ghulam Mohammad, Iskander Mirza, et al. Once in office, his emphasis was on the word 'benevolent' in the term 'benevolent despotism', and there are endless reports of his basically humane attitude and conduct. A clean and correct man himself, he inducted these attributes into his administration, which to this day is remembered as such. Notwithstanding this, historians will probably judge Ayub unkindly, and in my view unfairly, as being the first to derail democracy in Pakistan. It was not him alone, but a cabal of which he was a member. But he did emerge as the first Chief Martial Law Administrator—CMLA, an acronym which slipped out so easily from the lips of Pakistanis, as they were to become familiar with it in years to come. And there is subsequent autobiographical evidence to substantiate that he had been planning this coup for years.

Ayub's final days in office were filled with countrywide demonstrations and agitation. The political institutions that he had created in his attempt to seek popular legitimacy had crumbled to dust, and taken with them many of the paper tiger politicians that inhabited them. A battered and confused Ayub Khan, who, a decade ago, had boldly emerged from the horizon and moved into Pakistan as Chief Martial Law Administrator, then run the country, with a large measure of success for the best part of that period, was now compelled to hand over the reins of power to his chosen successor, Army Chief General Yahya Khan in 1969. Yahya abrogated the Constitution and promptly declared Martial Law. On thinking back, I feel that Ayub's was probably one of the most benign kinds of dictatorship ever known to the world. It was certainly devoid of harsh brutalities. He once told me that 'grass will always grow over a battlefield but never under the hangman's gallows' (an observation of doubtful horticultural validity, but wholly admirable as an expression of humane feelings).

As I thought over Ayub's ten-year rule and all its achievements, I recalled with a touch of sadness the wise assessment of Macaulay on the fall of an earlier public figure. 'He had been guilty of the offense which, of all offenses, is punished most severely: he had been over-praised; he had excited too warm an interest; and the public, with its usual justice, chastised him for its own folly'.

The disturbances in the country were sufficient preoccupation for Ayub, and excluded any possibility for my meeting him prior to my departure for Moscow. But later, on a visit to Islamabad for consultations, I was able to seek an audience, and was received by him at his private residence on a hill overlooking the capital. He was as always, warm, hospitable, and gracious. His illness, as well as the political stresses that he had endured over the past three months, had obviously taken their toll, and he looked tired and old. We talked a bit about Moscow, and I told him that the Soviet leadership, especially Kosygin, remembered him with affection. He asked me to reciprocate his sentiments to them, and we parted on that note. His eyes retained their gentleness, but had clearly lost all sparkle and fire. His last years were, I am told, truly miserable, like a hunted animal, living in terror of any act or acts unleashed by the vengeance of Bhutto. But when he died (in 1974), thousands of mourners defied official restrictions to attend his funeral and paid their last respects to a leader whom they loved and admired. And the Pakistan Army, of which he was the very embodiment, buried him with full military honours.

As I drove away from his house, I reflected on the brief halcyon days of his rule, and felt that despite his vision and his broad-minded outlook, Ayub had never quite moved out of the army cantonment. Even when clad in an impeccable three piece suit, or an *achkan* and *shalwar*, or kitted out for golf or shooting, Ayub had the upright bearing of an army officer. Whenever I was with him, I felt that I was in the presence of an impressive figure who, while exuding confidence, was never overbearing. By the same token, his attitude and thinking were not inflexible. However, I was not impressed by his intellectual calibre, which I thought quite average. Like all leaders, he had his share of personal vanity. One example of this was his promoting himself to the rank of Field Marshal, largely at the urging of sycophantic advisers. To my quiet amusement, it was also triggered, I suspect, by a Punjab Regimental commemorative ceremonial march-past led by Claude Auchinleck, its Honorary Colonel Commandant, who raised his Field Marshal's baton in salute whilst Ayub was obliged, as General, to respond from the stand with a hand salute.

But Ayub Khan did give us security, law and order, good governance, and economic prosperity.

Forsan et haec olim meminisse iuvabit.
(Someday it will be pleasant even to remember this.)

The Aeneid—Virgil

5

General Agha Mohammed
Yahya Khan: 1969–1971

On 25 March 1969, in his final extraconstitutional act, Ayub Khan hands over power to Army Chief Yahya Khan instead of Assembly Speaker Abdul Jabbar Khan. Martial Law declared once again. Decisive measures implemented. West Pakistan reconstituted into original provinces; freedom of press and media; political parties commence campaigning as election day announced; productive visit to the Soviet Union and acquisition of Pakistan's only steel mill; facilitator of Sino–US contact, a landmark feature in the geopolitical evolution of the century; proposal 'from a Head through a Head to a Head'. Pakistan's freest and fairest ever election successfully conducted; triumphs end and tragedy commences as East and West Pakistan are virtually split by the election results; the emergence of Mujib and Bhutto; Yahya unable to manage the downward spiral in politics; devastating typhoon in East Pakistan; followed by brutal military action; 'stumbled from miscalculation in March to misadventure in December'. Indian invasion of East Pakistan, humiliating surrender at Dacca, breakup of Pakistan and creation of Bangladesh; public anger shared by army officers; resignation, and senior military junta arranges for

hand over to Zulfikar Ali Bhutto as President, and first and
only civilian Chief Martial Law Administrator.

General Yahya Khan's tenure was marked by turbulence
from beginning to end, but it encompassed two events
of international historic significance, in both of which
he played a critical role. The first was his contribution,
initially embryonic and subsequently substantial, in
the establishment of diplomatic relations between the
United States of America and the People's Republic of
China. It was to lead to a fundamental change in the
international political alignment of the mid-twentieth
century, a development whose importance can never be over
emphasized. The second was the disintegration of Pakistan,
leading to the creation of Bangladesh, an event that also
made its impact on the world scene, but in a much more
bloody and destructive fashion, and in which Yahya's role
was by no means less significant.

Shortly after the declaration of Martial Law, I was back
in Islamabad for consultations and could see how Yahya's
early, decisive actions had eliminated the uncertainty and
floundering of the final days of the Ayub regime. One Unit
had been disbanded and autonomy restored to the four
provinces of West Pakistan. The press had been rendered
totally free and the electronic media, which, at that time,
constituted only the state-run radio and television, had been
made available to all politicians, and had been constantly
and vigorously used and exploited by the leaders of all the
political parties. Although a date had not yet been set for
General Elections, there was certainty that the country

was set in that direction. Despite the air of freedom that prevailed, I could discern some disquieting trends: not only was there a pronounced difference in attitudes between East and West Pakistan, but this gap was already being widened by the demagoguery of Zulfikar Ali Bhutto and Sheikh Mujibur Rahman; rather than making any attempt at reconciliation, each was exploiting these differences for their own political ends. However, these differences had not yet completely vitiated the political atmosphere of the country, and when Yahya left for Moscow, the domestic situation was comparatively peaceful, with him very much in control, and indeed, enjoying a measure of popular support.

I had first met Yahya Khan in Quetta in August 1947, when he was a Major and a senior Muslim officer in the garrison at the time. We celebrated the independence of Pakistan at a tremendous party at the Quetta Club, and Yahya made a speech entirely appropriate to the occasion. Since then, our meetings had been infrequent but always pleasant, and thus our meeting in the autumn of 1969 was the first time that I was able to have a substantial interaction with Yahya Khan. I discerned that behind the bluff and hearty manner, coupled with an earthy soldierly bearing, there was an intelligent and decisive mind. He gave a sober account of the situation in the country, and had no illusions of the difficulties that confronted him. He gave me no specific instructions regarding my forthcoming assignment, but said he intended to visit Moscow as soon as possible. 'They were the first to give me an official invitation and I intend to avail of it as soon as possible'.

For me, quite naturally, the immediate concern was Pakistan-USSR relations, and in this respect, as I read the files and absorbed the briefings from the Foreign Office, I found that things were remarkably equitable, and there appeared to be some interesting opportunities for development. Our close ties to China and, less so, to the USA, not to mention the Soviet ties to India, would always be impediments, but it was possible to work around them. The recent visit to the Soviet Union by President Ayub Khan had been a resounding success, and he had even been able to obtain Soviet military hardware, including tanks, much to the chagrin of India. However, after the initial delivery, supplies were suspended, and as we correctly suspected, this was linked with the departure of Ayub. The Foreign Office thought that I should make the resumption of military assistance my first priority when I got to Moscow, but I differed, sensing that the Soviets would prefer to see how the internal political situation developed in Pakistan before they made any commitments on sensitive items like tanks and guns. I therefore proposed that our priority should be the steel mill, and with the concurrence of Foreign Secretary S. M. Yusuf, we worked in that direction. The history of Pakistan's efforts to acquire a steel mill had been very chequered, with the breakdown of negotiations with two different western groups, and an unwise rebuff of a previous Soviet offer. It was quite clear that the Soviets were aware of our predicament when we reopened negotiations, and we decided to adopt a strategy that would be realistic and dignified, devoid of both apology and bluster. Yusuf, with his high intelligence and cool temperament, was the ideal chief negotiator, who eventually led the project to fulfilment.

In our preparatory meetings in Islamabad for Yahya's official visit to the Soviet Union, it was decided that we should concentrate on political issues and economic cooperation, whilst downplaying the matter of the interrupted military supplies. The composition of the President's delegation for the USSR visit reflected this decision and consisted of the Finance Minister, the Chairmen of the Planning Commission and the Steel Mill, the Secretary and Director General from the Foreign Office. The only military personnel were Major General Ghulam Omer, Chairman National Security Council, and Brigadier Ishaq, the eccentric Military Secretary to the President. As far as other items that could come up for discussion with the Soviets were concerned, the most sensitive was the issue of Tashkent, which was very close to Kosygin's heart, but which had by now become a focal point in Bhutto's agitation against the government, and had contributed in no small measure to the downfall of Ayub. I suggested to Yahya that he would need to tread carefully around this one, perhaps by singling out and lavishing praise on the Lenin Centenary.

Yahya was greeted on arrival at the Vnukovo International Airport in Moscow by a high-powered Soviet delegation. It included President Podgorny, Prime Minister Kosygin, Defence Minister Marshal Grechko, Deputy Foreign Minister Firyubin and a number of other officials. As the Kremlin apartments were under repair, Yahya was lodged in one of the Czar's palaces situated on the outskirts of Moscow, and was driven there in the company of his distinguished hosts. Upon arrival, we were presented with the sort of tremendous feast that only the Soviets can provide, and which evoked the intended gastronomical response from their chief guest, who tucked into it with cheerful gusto. The atmosphere was lively and convivial, and Podgorny and Kosygin each took it in turn to toast Yahya with glasses of vodka. The Soviet leaders were of course aware of their guest's propensity for alcohol, and I was amazed and a trifle disgusted that these world leaders would start a state visit with such a cheap and shoddy prank. But Yahya, who was obviously aware of these tactics, turned up trumps and said after the fourth toast, 'Mister President, Mister Prime Minister, I feel that this is not very fair. I know what you are trying to do, but there are only two of you against me, and that is not fair for you. I warn you that I can easily handle four of you.' At that Kosygin laughed, threw up his hands, and promptly put his upended glass on the table. After that, conversation was resumed in a more serious manner.

There was a formal dinner, hosted by Kosygin in the Kremlin's opulent Czarist banquet hall, and attended by senior Soviet officials and the Pakistani delegation. Conversation at the dinner was frank and wide-ranging, but Yahya's formal speech did not quite satisfy Kosygin. After the President had concluded his speech, Kosygin remarked wryly that Yahya had made a great many laudatory references to the Lenin Centenary, which was being celebrated that year in the Soviet Union, but had hardly said a word about the Tashkent Declaration.

The next day, there was an official meeting of both delegations in the Kremlin. Podgorny continued on the same topic with an ominous statement, 'Mr President, let me inform you that Prime Minister Kosygin has hitched his star to Tashkent, and we regard its implementation as central to our relations.' Yahya did a very good job at evading the issue, although he did clearly and frankly give an account of the prevailing political situation in Pakistan and of the measures that he intended to take, including a free election. Kosygin followed this with great interest, and was exceedingly forthcoming on our next topic, which was the steel mill. Here again, Yahya proved to be a skilled negotiator. He was clear in his objectives, flexible in his approach, and cloaked it all in a cloud of bluff heartiness. We got the steel mill on very favourable terms. It had been a successful session, and Yahya had studiously avoided all reference to arms deliveries, an omission that somewhat mystified the Soviets.

At the conclusion of the official visit in Moscow, the delegation was taken to Leningrad for two days. As we boarded the luxurious special train for our overnight return to Moscow, we were informed that Podgorny and Kosygin would meet Yahya at the train station and drive with him to the Vnukovo airport. Over dinner in the train that night, Fomin, a senior official in the Soviet Foreign Ministry and the KGB, approached me and said the Soviet leaders had been surprised that Yahya had not raised the issue of resumption of arms supplies with them. 'Do you not think that important? If you do, then the President should be advised to raise it with the Soviet leaders when he meets them in the morning.' I immediately went to Yahya Khan's saloon, where he and his coterie, now thoroughly relaxed, were at the height of a drinking party, and conveyed this important message. At the same time, Yusuf came in and conveyed the gist of a similar talk that he had just had with Degtyar, the Soviet Ambassador to Pakistan. Yahya immediately dismissed his drinking companions, as well as the fumes of alcohol from his mind, summoned Foreign Secretary Sultan Khan, and very lucidly conducted a strategy session for the meeting next morning. He then went back to his party.

The next morning, there was a long delay at the Vnukovo airport, with the Presidential Zil limousine parked at the gangway to the PIA aircraft whilst its three distinguished occupants, Yahya, Podgorny, and Kosygin, were engaged in deep discussion. They finally emerged, smiling broadly, and before boarding the plane Yahya thanked me for making his visit successful, adding that the Foreign Secretary would send me a signal for future course of action. It arrived duly, instructing me to request the Soviets to reactivate the arms supplies, as agreed in the talks held between Yahya and the two Soviet leaders. But when my approaches at the administrative level met with no response, I took up the issue with Kosygin. Assuming his best avuncular attitude, the Soviet Prime Minister advised us to concentrate on economic development and 'not to accelerate the matter' of arms deliveries. My telegram to Islamabad reporting this discouraging conversation provoked the expected shock waves of outrage and indignation. I did not know at the time that Yahya Khan, in the first flush of his return from Moscow, had already informed the senior officers at the GHQ that Soviet weapons supplies would soon be resumed. This unexpected volte-face obviously cut Yahya to the quick, and rightly infuriated him. I am still not able to find an explanation for this bizarre episode. Why nudge us into asking for arms when we had decided not to, in the first place? And then blandly turn down our request?

As part of their Cold War strategy, the Soviets had lured a number of young people from Asian and African countries with the promise of an education. These included some Pakistani boys who had entered the USSR without any documents and were lodged in the Patrice Lumumba University, where they had acquired little beyond a rudimentary knowledge of the Russian language, and the elements of Marxism-Leninism. They were disillusioned, cold, hungry, and miserably homesick. At the end of Yahya's visit to Moscow, he graciously asked if there was anything he could do for me. I informed him of the plight of these students and asked for his permission to issue them with Pakistani Passports so that they could go home. Yahya's response was typical: generosity replete with expletives. 'Give the silly buggers their bloody passports, and a kick on their arses at the same time.'

With agreements on the steel mill, the five-year trade plan, and the establishment of a high-level political dialogue in place, President Yahya's visit to the USSR was hailed as a success by the controlled press in both countries. In a typically flamboyant gesture, which touched me greatly, Yahya announced that he had awarded me the Sitara-i-Quaid-i-Azam (SQA). The actual presentation took place at a private occasion at the Government House, Karachi. There, Yahya also spoke about his fondness for and his collection of St Bernard dogs, being aware that my family also possessed these splendid and beautiful animals. After the ceremony, which Diana also attended, Yahya very deferentially ('I don't want to force it on you') offered me one of his pups. Hence, we came home with an SQA and Saint Cecelia, the puppy!

About a year later, I was in Islamabad, and was present at a banquet given by President Yahya in honour of a Chinese delegation that had just signed an agreement establishing the Heavy Industries Complex in Taxila. It was perhaps the most embarrassing function that I have ever attended. Yahya and his generals, as well as civilian 'advisers', were quite drunk, whilst their distinguished Chinese guests, as sober as their hosts were inebriated, displayed a bland and polite, if somewhat puzzled look. We were very close to a war with India, and while the toasts raised by the Chinese guests appropriately stressed Sino-Pakistan cooperation, and the success of the joint industrial project that had just been completed, the speeches by the Pakistani hosts consisted largely of bellicose threats addressed to India, and to Indira Gandhi in particular. 'We send you a message, loud and clear,' etc. etc. (There is no evidence to suggest

that the lady was in any way terrified, either then or later.)
In the middle of his rambling speech, Yahya expressed his
disappointment and frustration with the Soviets also for
'failing in their promises', a reference to the arms cut-off
that had obviously caused him embarrassment. A friend
of mine, seated beside me at the dinner, said 'there goes
your steel mill'. But he was mistaken: the Soviets stuck
to their word and were true to their commitment. I left
for Moscow the next morning in a deeply troubled state,
disgusted by the display at the dinner and astonished by
the irresponsibility and depravity to which alcohol had
reduced my Head of State. This was not the competent
Yahya Khan that I had known and got on so well with in
Moscow a year earlier.

An attractive and amusing aspect of Yahya's idiosyncratic
behaviour was in his relations with his Military Secretary,
Brigadier Ishaq, a deeply religious man, who said his prayers
regularly, and abstained from alcohol. Trim and fit as a
parachutist must be, the latter also had his share of quirks,
one of which was to never sit at his desk, but to work on
his files whilst standing at the lectern especially provided
for him in his office. The contrast between President and
his Military Secretary, in terms of attitudes, bearing, and
deportment, could not have been more striking. But despite
this, they worked in closest harmony. Despite the difference
in their outward conduct, Yahya and Ishaq were clearly
devoted to each other. Whenever I saw them together,
which was quite often, I thought of Don Quixote and
Sancho Panza.

During one of my consultation visits to Islamabad from Moscow, I was summoned by Yahya for a personal meeting. He said that the subject which he was about to discuss with me was highly confidential, and the only reason that he was divulging it to me was 'because you are sitting on top of a bloody volcano and need to know about it'. He mentioned the top secret initiatives that were underway for a US-China rapprochement and of his personal role in this fascinating exercise. Yahya said that he was currently working on a secret visit by Kissinger to Beijing. All communications between him and Nixon were through handwritten letters in order to ensure complete security. He said it had commenced at the Governor's House, Lahore, where Yahya and Nixon had their first meeting in August 1969. According to Yahya, Nixon said to him, 'Mr President, both you and I have just taken over office as President, so I think that you and I can learn a lot from each other. Tell me, what do you think of our China policy?' Yahya's response was short and pithy. 'All bloody wrong. How can you ignore such a large nation with so many people? We have differences in religion and culture and yet have the best relations with them.'

In the discussions that followed, Nixon, Kissinger, and Yahya planned the early modus operandi that first took Kissinger in secret in a PIA aircraft to Peking. This was followed by Nixon's visit to China and the signature of the Shanghai Agreement on 28 February 1972, an event that created a watershed in mid-twentieth century international relations. The essence of this unique diplomatic exchange was later summed up in Chinese Prime Minister Zhou En-lai's famous expression, 'From a Head, through a Head, to a Head'. It underlines the crucial role played by Yahya: first, for his part in persuading Nixon to initiate a change in the US's China policy; next, in conveying it to Beijing as realistic; and finally, in providing in secret the vital logistic requirements for the project. Above all, in the crude, outspoken, but sharp ruffian soldier that was Yahya Khan, the leaders of both China and the United States—the former being an ancient oriental civilization and the latter a sophisticated technologically-driven western society—found a person in whom they could place their implicit trust.

But this *batailles des fleurs* of the two superpowers carried some devastating consequences for its choreographer, Pakistan. As Yahya had correctly anticipated, I had been sitting on a bloody volcano, but when it erupted, the fallout was more serious for him than it was for me. The Soviets reacted by signing a Friendship Treaty with India (the only non-communist country with which they did so) and then embarked upon an implacable series of diplomatic and military actions against Pakistan, leading up to and including the war in East Pakistan. When it was all over, and I was discussing the events with Professor Yuri V. Gankovsky, a senior Soviet official and a good personal friend, he said to me 'my dear Marker, why did Kissinger have to go to Beijing from Islamabad? He could have gone from Hong Kong or Bangkok, or any other place. This visit has done much more harm to our relations than even the U-2 flight.' (Gankovsky was referring to the American U-2 spy plane which had flown from its secret base near Peshawar and had been shot down over the Soviet Union on 7 May 1960, with the capture of its infamous pilot, Gary Powers. The repercussions of the incident included the cancellation of an Eisenhower-Khurschev summit, Khurschev's shoe thumping at the UN General Assembly debate, and his threat to the Pakistan Ambassador that Peshawar had been 'circled in red' on his map.)

Despite Yahya's beneficial efforts in the international arena, his handling of the situation in Pakistan—which had started in such deft fashion—meant the country was now in utter ruin. It moved from one disaster to another, the only redeeming feature being the General Elections that were held in 1971. These were, without doubt, the freest and fairest elections ever held in Pakistan. They were perfectly organized and conducted, so much so, that Henry Kissinger is reported to have said in his inimitable fashion to Yahya, 'Mr President, for a military dictator, you run a lousy election'.

The initial reports provided to the junta by the military and civil intelligence agencies predicted electoral victories by multiple parties, thus enabling Yahya to play the kingmaker. As usual, the spooks had reported to their masters what the masters liked to hear, and both had come a cropper. Faced with the stark electoral result, with one party holding an overwhelming majority in each wing of the country, Yahya was at first furious, and then began to fumble his unknowing way through a political jungle. I met him several times during this difficult period, as our deteriorating relations with the Soviet Union compelled me to visit Islamabad quite often on fire-fighting missions. I kept him informed of the increasing Soviet hostility towards Pakistan, but by this time it had no palpable effect.

The Shah of Iran, Reza Shah Pahlavi, had decided to mark the centennial of the Iranian monarchy with a grandiose celebration arranged in a grand, opulent, and vulgar ceremony at the ancient and spectacular ruins of Persepolis. A number of Heads of State had been invited and each had been lodged in a luxurious tent. Yahya Khan and Podgorny and Kosygin were also present, and it was my understanding that the Shah of Iran (as a supplement to the dizzy heights of the megalomania that was manifest in the centenary celebrations) had wished to use his good offices to bring about an understanding between Pakistan and the USSR. My fading hopes were based on a positive outcome of a meeting, under the benign patronage of the Shahinshah, but these proved to be quite illusory. From the Foreign Ministry report of the meeting, which I received after much prompting, it was an unmitigated disaster. The Soviets were threatening and almost abusive, and Yahya was equally abusive and drunk. After that, it was downhill all the way. The Soviets fulfilled their commitments to India under their Friendship Treaty, and I sat around helpless in Moscow as I witnessed Pakistan being torn apart. The last time that I saw Yahya was the day that I left Islamabad for Moscow, which was also the day war broke out. He walked into his office, wearing civilian clothes but carrying his swagger stick, looking serious, absorbed, and slightly puzzled. He wished me good luck, and hoped that I had 'got some sun in your bones' during my visit to Pakistan. As I departed from the President's office, leaving Yahya in deep consultation with his advisers, I was filled with forebodings for the future of the country. They appeared neither to have known nor cared about the havoc and destruction they had caused in East Pakistan. Moreover, they seemed hell-bent on military action against India, which seemed to be reciprocating in an increasingly provocative fashion.

As I flew out of Pakistan, I recalled being informed by friends and colleagues of the frequent drunken parties deteriorating into wild parties at Yahya's home. I saw how this behaviour had told not only upon his health and appearance but also on his thinking and judgement. The final days of Pakistan and the creation of Bangladesh have been recorded by historians, and retold by many of those who actually participated in these historic events. It is therefore well beyond the ambit of this particular presentation, which is a personal recollection of events as I saw them, and impressions obtained as I moved, in those dreadful days, between Islamabad, Karachi, and Moscow. I observed, with concern, how the single-minded and selfish will of two obsessive politicians, Zulfikar Ali Bhutto and Mujibur Rahman, each determined in their own way to resist any compromise, proved to be well beyond any statesmanship that Yahya might be able to muster at this late stage of his confused leadership.

I saw Pakistan stumble into the disastrous military action in East Pakistan. 'Thank God, Pakistan has been saved!' shrieked a triumphant Bhutto, after he had manoeuvred a wavering and fumbling Yahya into using force, and killing innocent—and sometimes not so innocent—Bengalis to impose a military solution. This eventually turned into a bitter ethnic conflict, which inevitably led to a massive Indian intervention and the shameful surrender at the Dacca racecourse. History has recorded the dramatic events that sent Bhutto to the United Nations in New York, the deliberately frustrated telephone conversations over the Polish Draft Resolution that preceded the end of the conflict, and Bhutto's return to Pakistan under a military umbrella. During this period, I remained in Moscow, incarcerated by events, a helpless and frustrated witness to the unfolding tragedy.*

As an American Ambassador succinctly put it in one of his contemporary despatches, Yahya had 'stumbled from miscalculation in March to misadventure in December'. Or else, as Henry Kissinger said to me when we discussed these events years later in New York, 'In most countries of the world, elections help to solve problems. In Pakistan they seem to create them.'

I never saw Yahya Khan again, although I did get news of him from time to time. He passed his last days under house arrest, lonely and sad, and although not a contemplative

---

Quiet Diplomacy: Memoirs of an Ambassador of Pakistan by Jamsheed Marker (Karachi: Oxford University Press, 2010).

man by nature, I wondered how he had viewed his life and achievements in his final years. Did the awareness ever fully dawn on him, that he played a crucial and positive role in the adjustment of world history in the mid-twentieth century? And by the same token, despite his evidence before the Hamudur Rehman Commission (that was set up by the Government of Pakistan in 1972 to prepare a complete account of the atrocities committed in the 1971 war), did he ever really assess the full extent of his culpability in the final disaster that overwhelmed Pakistan? Finally, it needs to be said that whatever his other faults and failings, Yahya Khan was not a corrupt ruler. In terms of financial probity, his administration was perhaps as sound as any that we had since Liaquat Ali Khan. For a Pakistani leader, that is saying quite a lot!

The Pakistan created by Muhammad Ali Jinnah had ended in a painful, grisly, and bloody convulsion. And for this, Yahya Khan must bear considerable responsibility. After all, he was one of the trio—Zulfikar Ali Bhutto and Mujibur Rahman being the other two who engineered it.

During the course of my enquiries regarding Yahya Khan's welfare in his last days, I was informed that his guardians were surprised at the amount of meat that was being consumed in the household, and that its cost almost equalled his alcohol bill! From this, I concluded with the assurance that my fellow dog lover and friend, Raja Yahya, was taking good care of his St Bernards.

6

Zulfikar Ali Bhutto: 1971–1977

Zulfikar Ali Bhutto, President and Chief Martial Law Administrator (CMLA), played a leading role in bringing a country to defeat and despair, and then galvanized a dramatic recovery. The three achievements that took Bhutto's success to its zenith were: (a) the Simla Agreement with India in July 1972, a triumph of Bhutto's diplomatic skill, which resulted in the return of conquered Pakistan territories and Prisoners of War; (b) the energetic organization and conduct of the Islamic Conference at Lahore including, after some deft diplomatic moves, a resolution on Pakistan–Bangladesh recognition; (c) The passage through the National Assembly by near consensus in 1973 of a Constitution which changed the political structure of Pakistan, from a presidential to a parliamentary system and concentrated power in the office of the Prime Minister, which Bhutto assumed and exercised with customary lusty zeal. The decline of Bhutto's destiny was almost as meteoric as his rise, and commenced, as these things so often do, at the historical climax of his success. For no sooner had he achieved the seemingly impossible task of creating a system which gave him dictatorial powers under a democratic façade than he began to tinker with it. His first act was to dismiss the duly elected Balochistan government, a violation which immediately unleashed an angry protest that dogged the Bhutto government till the end of its term.

The self-destructive element, so characteristic of the Bhutto regime, began to cast its malign spell over the policies and direction upon which the country was forced to embark. Nationalization commenced with the larger industrial enterprises, then gobbled up medium institutions, and extended the absurdities to the tiniest projects, such as small cotton gins and oil-pressing plants in the countryside, where most owners lived in their workplaces and were thus dispossessed of both their livelihood and their homes by the petty bureaucrats appointed by the government to run their little mills. More importantly, with the nationalization of banks, the government, together with the bureaucrats, had secured through control of the instruments of financial credit, an increased stranglehold on the fabric of the administration of the country.

Almost as devastating was the nationalization in the field of education, where academic quality and standards were uprooted and replaced by quantities of the poorest and most deplorable of party hacks. But it was the civil administration that suffered the most disastrous consequences of Bhutto's rampage through the established order. Measures like the Lateral Entry Scheme poured incompetent sycophants from the Pakistan Peoples Party (PPP) into the Civil Service, raising nepotism to perhaps the most outrageous levels seen in the country before or since, and reducing standards of efficiency and probity in equally deplorable measure.

Most destructive, and ultimately damaging to its founder himself, was the creation of the Federal Security Force (FSF), a paramilitary praetorian guard subservient to Bhutto only, and clearly designed to counter the influence of the regular armed forces and the police. Its hand-picked commander was Masood Mahmood, an unprincipled, brutal, and sadistic police officer who later turned approver in the trial that led to Bhutto's execution.[2]

By the time he was half-way through his term of office, Bhutto was also half-way through his effort to turn Pakistan from a promising democracy into a personal fiefdom, filled with corrupt, grasping sycophants, and a society where the rule of law had been contemptuously discarded and was being methodically replaced by a crypto-dictatorship. But this was also the high-watermark of the Bhutto era, when his writ was unchallenged within the country and his dynamic charisma evoked enthusiasm abroad, marking him as a Third World leader of repute.

Then came the decline.

The exact moment of the ebb and flow in the tides of the fortunes of political movements and leaders is always imprecise, but in my view, the seeds of disintegration probably began with the dismissal of the elected Balochistan government: the popular resistance that it provoked dogged his government to its very end. As time went on, Bhutto's compulsive thrust for the acquisition of power brought with it successes as well as self-generated setbacks. The greatest of these was the surprise appointment of a hitherto unknown general as Chief of Army Staff: one whose conduct moved from initial subservience to a deadly rivalry that eventually fashioned a classic Greek tragedy.

Another was the ordinance to nationalize banks, which provided easy access to funds, but choked up the banking system; much the same happened in the case of all the other nationalized sectors, resulting in a disastrous overall setback to the economy. This in turn added to the existing general political opposition and to the build-up of resistance to government. An increasingly desperate Bhutto called for General Elections, which were blatantly rigged, and triggered massive public protest and demonstrations. In order to retrieve the situation, he commenced negotiating with the opposition parties, who, sensing the advantage of their position, became increasingly obdurate, and secured from Bhutto a series of unbelievable concessions, ranging from prohibition of alcohol to the declaration of Qadianis/ Ahmadis as non-Muslims. As the political parties remained locked in an internecine conflict, Bhutto floundered and flailed in a desperate last-ditch and unavailing attempt to save himself and his regime. He also simultaneously sounded the death knell of civilian government and laid the foundations of fundamentalism in Pakistan.

Then came Zia ul-Haq.

The epoch of Zulfikar Ali Bhutto remains indelibly imprinted in the history of Pakistan. Frequently regarded as 'a flawed genius', his life and work have been recorded by many authors: some are serious studies, others are

emotionally tinged biographies,[3] but for the most part
they are the usual collection of tracts, either hagiographic
or polemical. Not surprisingly, the bibliography on Z. A.
Bhutto, like its subject, remains extensive, varied, and
streaked with bloodshed and tragedy. It is not the purpose
of this book to add to the vast choice available to the
discerning reader. It is merely to recall the impression
gained from personal contacts and association with this
difficult but always fascinating personality. Like a comet,
it had suddenly emerged on the political constellation of
Pakistan, emblazoned it for a while, and just as dramatically
disappeared, consumed in the brilliant flames that it had
itself created.

Apart from his role in the breakup of Pakistan, two of
Bhutto's actions profoundly affected the ethos of the state
and its citizens. The first was that he provided reality
to the concept of vox populi: he did this by taking the
process of electioneering out of the drawing rooms of the
wealthy and into the streets of the populace. As a Pakistani
cab driver in New York later commented to me about
Bhutto, 'Sahib, iss nay humain zabaan dai dee' (Sir, he has
given us a voice). The second, much more destructive and
reprehensible, was the way in which Bhutto brought about
a fundamental change in the hitherto prevalent concept of
honesty in public life. He deliberately fostered an attitude
of amorality as being the norm, both in public life and
personal behaviour. His immediate entourage, selected by
himself, consisted of crude swaggering ruffians, sickening in
their obsequiousness to their leader and in their arrogance

to everyone else. This was reminiscent of the Nazi SS, and it did not end there.

In this connection, it would not be out of place to recall a letter written by Bhutto to Governor General Iskander Mirza, in which the ambitious young politician, desperately aspiring to high office, extols Mirza's leadership as superior to that of Quaid-i-Azam. Combining as it does the lowest depths of political flattery and obsequiousness, this missive leaves the reader breathless. (Knowing Iskander, it probably invoked a contemptuous snort.)

I first met Zulfikar Ali Bhutto just after he had returned to Pakistan from his studies abroad (Political Science at Berkeley, California; and Law at Oxford), and was introduced to him by our common friend, Omar Kureishi, with whom I was associated through cricket and broadcasting. Omar and Bhutto knew each other from their Cathedral School days in Bombay, and were later at Berkeley together. Omar, myself, and a number of friends, that included journalists, diplomats, businessmen, and budding politicians used to meet for informal lunches at the Coffee House on a regular basis. Omar introduced Bhutto to our group shortly after the former's return from abroad. Tall, friendly, witty, and obviously well-read and intelligent, 'Zulfi' as we all knew him then, made an immediate impact on everyone that he met. (I thought that in his handsome bearing one could detect a distinct trace of the Rajput nobility in his ancestry.) Bhutto and I began an easygoing friendship, which was warmed by our mutual love for cricket; he frequently joined us in the commentary box, and displayed both his enthusiasm and expertise of the game.

On arrival in Karachi, Bhutto, as a promising young lawyer, took up chambers at Wadhumal & Co., an old established legal firm of Karachi whose senior partner was Dingomal Narayansingh. In pre-Partition days, there was a closely-knit, multi-religious, and multiethnic elite in Sindh, consisting of landlords, businessmen, doctors, lawyers, and administrators. Sir Shahnawaz Bhutto and Dingomal Narayansingh, together with Sir Ghulam Husain Hidayatullah and Sir Abdullah Haroon, were members of this distinguished group who, along with other citizens of equal distinction, used to meet regularly at each other's homes and at the Karachi Club (Sindh Club membership being open to Europeans only). Zulfikar Bhutto's admission to the chambers of Wadhumal & Co. on return to Karachi was therefore almost a family affair—until the end of his life, Zulfikar used to address Dingomal as '*chacha*' (uncle). Under the umbrella of this distinguished familial and political patronage, Bhutto launched himself into politics and cultivated, in his own inimitable and vigorous fashion, a group of admirers.

In the late 1950s, politics in Pakistan had just begun its transformation from its free and rambunctious nature into the ordered form of an authoritarian regime. During this interim period, our Coffee House allegiances undertook some changes—Omar and Zulfi towards politics and me towards business. I also noticed a growing friendship and closeness between Iskander Mirza, the powerful and ambitious bureaucrat, and Zulfikar Bhutto, a dynamic and equally ambitious young lawyer. Iskander was quite clearly grooming Bhutto for greater jobs, and also, both men thought that each in their own fashion were on the cusp of power. In this they were right. Omar told me that shortly after Martial Law was proclaimed, he was approached by Bhutto who, as expected, had become part of the establishment. Omar told me, 'Grinning from ear to ear like a Cheshire cat, he [Bhutto] said, "This is it, boy! You are to take over *The Pakistan Times*!"' This was the newspaper that had prestigious personalities such as the legendary Faiz Ahmed Faiz and Mazhar Ali amongst its editors, and they had been summarily dismissed. Omar told me that he turned down the offer on the grounds that since he *shaved every day*, he would not be able to look himself in the mirror each morning.

Bhutto's political career continued to advance, first under the patronage of Iskander Mirza, who brought him to the attention of Ayub Khan, who in turn fell under the spell cast by the brilliance, charm, and flattery of Bhutto's engaging personality. Now that the Bhutto comet had made its entry in the sky, we saw less of him, but it was nevertheless enough to get to study and observe his operational methods. His sharp instincts had quickly sensed the power shift within the junta, and although Iskander had just nominated Bhutto as Pakistan's Representative to the UN Law of Sea Conference in Geneva, and then as a Member of the Pakistan delegation to the UN General Assembly in New York, we could sense that the young minister was already working his way into the Ayub orbit.

Bhutto was made Minister of Commerce and subsequently Minister of Fuel, Power, and National Resources, from whence he made a much self-publicized visit to Moscow to sign an 'oil agreement with the USSR'. Of course, at our Coffee House sessions we were regaled, ad nauseam, with the details of this monumental achievement. But I noted also how in due course, Bhutto's brilliance, coupled with his opportunism, asserted itself, and he literally shot up the ladder of political success. He had become a great favourite of the Ayub family (and of Begum Ayub Khan in particular), and for a few years his star was firmly in the ascendancy, leading to his cherished appointment as Foreign Minister.

I did not have too much contact with Bhutto during this period, but whilst rejoicing in his successes, there was also concern about his increased arrogance and recklessness. However, in the years 1964–65, our paths crossed in a much more definite fashion. Fate moved both of us from Coffee House socializing to the Ministry of Foreign Affairs, and we assumed the protocol and role appropriate to the relationship between Minister and Ambassador. Although a comparative novice in the field of foreign affairs, it immediately became clear to me that Bhutto had begun to place the unmistakable stamp of his ideas and personality on a hitherto staid and tradition-bound Foreign Office. (For example, he eliminated the custom, in official communications between Ambassadors and the

Foreign Minister, of the pompous suffix 'Esquire', and any titles, after the name of the recipient, and replacing it with a simple 'Mr'.) By the time that I had joined the Foreign Ministry, Bhutto's imprint had developed well beyond the formalities and into substantive policy issues. The institution not only possessed a left-leaning incline but appeared set on a clear leftist course under the enthusiastic direction of its new Foreign Minister. Personal friendships and associations were pursued with newly emerging Third World leaders like Sukarno, Nasser, Nkrumah, and Tito (although Nehru's presence posed an awkward obstacle to Bhutto's attempt to join this jolly band of brothers). This shift in policy was the subject of an increasingly intensive debate, not only within the government, but also abroad, and provided me with an opportunity to observe, as a Foreign Ministry official, the style and manner of Bhutto's political skill and daring which he pitted against his rivals, both foreign and domestic.

In 1965, I left Pakistan in order to assume my first diplomatic assignment as High Commissioner to Ghana, a move that kept me in a career that lasted over thirty years.[4]

My relations with Bhutto, as already indicated, became increasingly infrequent and formal. While I was involved in following events in the early period of African independence, in itself a most fascinating diplomatic pursuit, Bhutto was playing a key role in the important political developments in the Indo-Pakistan subcontinent, which subsequently led to the war in Kashmir, followed by the Tashkent Agreement. They are issues of historical record, as are those of the many analyses by qualified historians that have followed. My purpose is to report the events of the era as seen by a distant, but by no means uninterested observer.

By now, the fallout between President Ayub Khan and his erstwhile favourite, the Foreign Minister Bhutto, was common knowledge, their differences over policy having deteriorated into bitter personal acrimony. ('This bloody Field Marshal has the mind of a Sergeant Major,' Bhutto is reported to have once unjustly and unwisely observed.) Shortly before I received my orders of transfer from Accra in Ghana to Bucharest, we heard the news of Bhutto's dismissal as Foreign Minister. This made me a little sad, as I thought that he had done an effective job. I wrote him a letter telling him so, and expressing the belief that he would do a great deal more for Pakistan in the future. He was kind enough to reply to me in reciprocal friendly terms. Little could we have foreseen, in the summer of 1967, as we exchanged this amicable correspondence, what the future held for each of us!

Bhutto's removal from the Foreign Ministry brought about a degree of stability to the institution, even though its new custodians, Foreign Minister Sharifuddin Pirzada and Foreign Secretary S. M. Yusuf, were not always in full accord. Pirzada remained, as ever, the consummate pragmatist, whilst Yusuf was amongst the most competent Foreign Secretaries that ever held the post: between them, they carried out a steady, calibrated implementation of Ayub's policy directives. This included a course correction, distinctly to the right, carried out without any dramatic flare.

Meanwhile, from the distance of my foreign postings in Bucharest and Moscow, which were interspersed with visits to Pakistan, I followed the misfortunes and fortunes of Bhutto, from the shattered and tearful moment of his sacking by Ayub, through his courageous recovery, to the establishment of the Pakistan Peoples Party (PPP) that Bhutto founded in 1967 and the hopes that it brought to so many in the country. I was moved by the liberal ideas contained in the Party Manifesto, and more so by the response that it was just beginning to evoke in the country.

During that period, I happened to be in Karachi, and made a customary call on ZAB (as Bhutto was called) at his baronial residence at 70 Clifton, where, apart from his family hangers-on, there seemed to be very few 'public' (as was expressively described in the local jargon). Bhutto was in an anxious and contemplative mood. He had just launched his party, and was in dire need of support, recognition, and above all, funds. In East Pakistan, Maulana Bhashani and Mujibur Rahman's strides, looming ominously over the political horizon, had added considerably to Bhutto's agitation and concern. I promised him a financial contribution, which in those days was both timely and substantial: his quiet, muted acknowledgement remained a shadowy, indefinable element in our subsequent personal relations.

But all this was to disappear and be carried away by the tempestuous events that followed: the bonhomie that had hitherto existed amongst us was replaced by an atmosphere of tension, often intense, as Bhutto's meteoric career pursued its turbulent way, losing friends and gaining enemies. I found myself in disagreement with a lot of his policies, and noted with increasing concern that his personal arrogance and intolerance had become a part of his political credo. The liberality of his party had been brutally discarded, and as he increased power in Pakistan, he resolutely set about creating a dictatorship, with all the trappings and instruments of a fascist regime. By this time, I had come to have the most profound doubts about Bhutto's policies and his conduct of the affairs of state, and very seriously considered a resignation. But two compelling reasons prevented me exercising the option at that time: the first was that I had already resigned (on principle, as I always did, when there was a change of government) and had not only been forcibly rebuffed by Bhutto, but also been persuasively urged by friends like Aziz Ahmed, who was now Foreign Minister, to remain in office. However, a further compulsion was that my wife, Diana, had been diagnosed with cancer, and needed to continue with the treatment that she had been undergoing in Germany. Accordingly, I gratefully accepted postings to Ottawa, East Berlin, and Tokyo, where there were reasonable medical facilities. These also kept me out of Bhutto's way. Diana passed away on 4 January 1979.

My only substantive contact with Bhutto was in Moscow at the end of my tenure, and at the conclusion of his successful official visit to the Soviet Union. Details of it have been covered in my book.[5] Here I need only refer to a personal conversation that I had with Bhutto, who was in a relaxed mood at the end of the successful visit. He started the conversation by saying, with that famous mischievous smile on his face, 'So in the end it was a bloody Parsi [referring to the Indian General Sam Maneckshaw who was Chief of Staff at the time of the 1971 Indo-Pak War] who defeated us.' I was not aware of it at the time, but I could have added to this, 'and also "a bloody Sikh" (Indian General Aurora), and a "bloody Jew" (Indian General Jacob)'. Becoming serious, he asked me what I thought of the visit. I said to him that in my opinion Kosygin still remained sceptical, but with Brezhnev, he had made a real breakthrough in restoring our relations with the USSR, and that was what really mattered.

I then said to him, 'Mr President, what you have said implies courage and a radical change in our policies. How do you think it can be done?'

He replied, 'You are only a bloody diplomat. *Tum yeh siyasati kaam nahin samajhtai ho* (you do not understand political practice). I shall take with me to India a delegation of about thirty MPs. They can go rollicking in New Delhi while their wives go shopping for saris. In the meantime, I will work out my agreement with Indira Gandhi, and when they return to Islamabad they will have to endorse it.' This tactic was reminiscent of US President Lyndon B. Johnson's view on dealing with recalcitrant members of the Congress.

During the situation that prevailed over the next decade, my only contacts with Bhutto were at the opulent Envoys' Conference in Rome, which produced nothing whatsoever in terms of substance, but was a monumental and extravagant exercise in perpetuating the Bhutto personality cult. This was, in general, the leitmotif of the political course being imposed upon the nation by Bhutto as he vigorously and ruthlessly began to mould it into a fascist state.

Historians of varying abilities and political affiliations have described the dramatic decade of Bhutto's regime—the triumph of the Islamic Conference in Lahore (popularly known as the Lahore Summit) in 1974, which could be truly described as a diplomatic and organizational tour de force that pulled Pakistan out of the morass of the Bangladesh disaster into the forefront of leadership of the Islamic nations. Yet alongside the shining symbols of the international successes in which Pakistan was basking, there lurked in this divine garden the legendary and ominous viper whose presence was impossible to conceal. Bhutto's megalomania had asserted itself and assumed all the accoutrements of fascism. Secret concentration camps were set up, and a praetorian guard, the Federal Security Force (FSF), under the sole command of Bhutto, was established for both aims: to take care of those unfortunates incarcerated, and to simultaneously pose a counter to the legitimate state security institutions, the police and the army. Later, these objectives were achieved with a grim ironic success, when the head of the FSF, the sadistic

Quaid-i-Azam Muhammad Ali Jinnah, circa July 1948

*Receives a delegation from the Quetta Parsi Anjuman, led by
Kekobad Marker, father of author.*
*Note the sartorial contrasts depicted in the photograph. The members of the delegation
clad in their obligatory formal Parsi garb, are in an awkward perch. Mr Jinnah, in his
impeccable Savile Row suit, retains his nonchalance and elegance.*

Prime Minister Liaquat Ali Khan and Begum Ra'ana Liaquat Ali Khan
at the Prime Minister's House, 10 Victoria Road, Karachi, circa 1951

*The Press Information Department had commissioned a prominent foreign
photographer to make an official portrait of the Prime Minister and Begum Liaquat.
As was customary at the time, the 'prominent foreign personality' was provided with a
Pakistani assistant/escort—in this case, an enthusiastic young photographer from the
Department. Whilst the distinguished foreigner was fussing around his subjects, the
young Pakistani took this delightful shot of Liaquat and Ra'ana.
It was the photograph that they chose,
and subsequently distributed to their friends.*

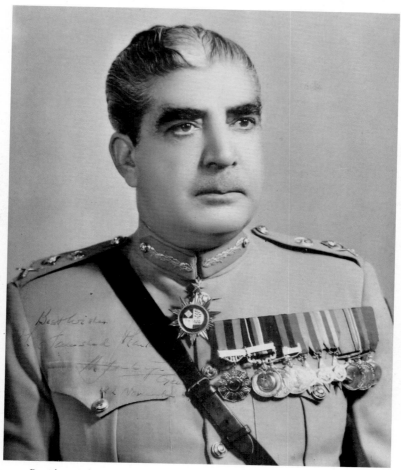

President Agha Mohammad Yahya Khan, March 1969–December 1971

Yahya Khan's moment of triumph: A key role in the conciliation between the USA and the Peoples Republic of China: 'From a Head, Through a Head, to a Head'—Zhou En-lai. Free and fair General Elections in Pakistan: outright victories for the Awami League and the Pakistan Peoples Party.' For a military dictator you run a lousy election, Mr President'—Henry Kissinger's remark to Yahya Khan.

Vnukovo Airport, Moscow, June 1970
Reception Committe awaiting the arrival of President Yahya Khan

*Left to right: Soviet Prime Minister Kosygin, Soviet Defence Minister Marshal Grechko,
Soviet President Podgorny, Qadri (Pakistan Foreign Ministry), M. Degteyar (Soviet
Ambassador to Pakistan), Jamsheed Marker, Major General Ghulam Umer (Chief of
Staff to President Yahya Khan), USSR Deputy Foreign Minister Nikolai Firyubin.
An unusually high-level reception committee which preceded a warm and successful
presidential visit. 'Just wait, my friends', I heard one cynic guest say,
'In three months they will come to us with folded hands
and say 'for God's sake take us back!'*

Official visit by President Bhutto, the Kremlin, Moscow, March 1972

Front row, left to right: Soviet Foreign Minister Gromyko, Soviet Prime Minister Aleksei Kosygin, President Z. A. Bhutto.

Rear row, left to right: Dr M. A. Bhatti, Ambassador Aftab Ahmed Khan (both from Pakistan Foreign Office), Saeed Ahmed (Governor, State Bank of Pakistan), Jamsheed Marker, Foreign Secretary Sultan Khan, M. M. Ahmed, Deputy Chairman, Planning Commission. A somewhat frosty meeting, which nevertheless became a precursor to the Simla Agreement.

Marker Cottage, Quetta, circa 1942

Diana, Hugo, and Khursheed on the front verandah.
This building replaced the one that had been our family home since 1895 and was
destroyed in the great earthquake of 1935. The architect was Andrew Grunberg, a
Jewish Hungarian refugee from Nazi oppression. The bungalow is in the Bauhaus
style, originally designed by the famous Walter Gropious, and a well-known feature of
contemporary European architecture. Marker Cottage in Quetta is probably the only
Bauhaus extant in South Asia. Hugo was obtained by Minoo, and was the first of a line
of St. Bernard dogs associated with the Marker Cottage.

President Yahya Khan, Governor's House, Karachi, 1971
Yahya is decorating the author with the Sitara-e-Quaid-i-Azam.
Diana attended the ceremony.

Bhutto and Brezhnev meet at the Kremlin, Moscow 1972

From left to right: Leonid Brezhnev, Secretary General, Communist Party of the Soviet Union, Andrey Gromyko, Soviet Foreign Minister, Andrey Rodionov, Soviet Ambassador to Pakistan. Jamsheed Marker, Pakistan Ambassador to the USSR, Pakistan Foreign Minister Aziz Ahmed, President of Pakistan Zulfikar Ali Bhutto. An important meeting that changed the course of history in South Asia.

Field Marshal Mohammad Ayub Khan

Military dictatorship followed by benevolent despotism. The Ayub Khan era has been regarded as a truly halcyon period in the history of Pakistan.
He was also subject to constant flattery. At the end of his visit to Romania he met with his senior officials, and dictated a telegram to Islamabad, reporting discussions and issuing instructions. He ended by saying to all of us, 'That covers it, don't you think?' This was loudly approved by all present except myself, who thought that Ayub had overlooked an important matter, and I said so. This provoked outrage among the courtiers: 'President Sahib has himself dictated the telegram! No need for change!' Ignoring the indignation, and correcting the text, Ayub softly said to me, 'Does this meet your requirement, ambassador?'

With my very best wishes and regards to my friend
Ambassador Jamsheed Marker

17 April 1985

President General Zia ul-Haq, July 1977–August 1988

A hitherto unknown general who came to exercise perhaps the most profound effect on the ethos, constitution, and destiny of Pakistan.

General Pervez Musharraf, October 1999–March 2008

Well-intentioned and progressive ideas bring considerable benefits to the country, particularly in the agricultural and technological sectors. There was notable peace and economic stability during the early period of the administration. This was later disturbed by brusque attempts to dominate the institutions of the judiciary (the courts) and the legislature (the National Assembly), and concluded with the disastrous National Reconciliation Ordinance.

Prime Minister Muhammad Khan Junejo, 1985–1988
Honest and incorruptible, but a poor statesman.
'When are you going to lift martial law, Mr President?'
The mouse that roared.

Ghulam Ishaq Khan, August 1988–July 1993

Greatest of administrators and sincerest of patriots.
Too reticent and retiring for the successful exercise of public office.

Prime Minister Benazir Bhutto, Washington DC, July 1989
Bhutto dedicates the new Chancery Premises of the Embassy of Pakistan
From left to right: Arnaz Marker, Jamsheed Marker, Prime Minister Benazir Bhutto.

Aiwan-e-Sadar, Islamabad, 2004
President Pervez Musharraf presents Jamsheed Marker with the Hilal-e-Imtiaz.

Non-Aligned Conference, Havana, Cuba, 1979

Pakistan Delegation led by President Zia ul-Haq.
from left to right: Ambassador Iqbal Akhund, Foreign Minister Agha Shahi,
Ambassadors Niaz Naik, Jamsheed Marker, President
Zia-ul-Haq, Ambassador Najmul Saquib, General K. M. Arif,
Chief of Staff to the President.

The Very Early Years
Pakistan's currency was a rubber stamp on a British Indian hundred rupee note.
Courtesy: Citizens Archives of Pakistan (CAP).

Masood Mahmood, turned approver in the trial that led to the execution of Zulfikar Ali Bhutto in 1979. In 1976, the FSF consisted of 18,000 men equipped with automatic weapons, grenades, rocket launchers, and hundreds of vehicles.

Encouraged by these successes, Bhutto embarked upon the systematic destruction of almost all the institutions that provided a modicum of security and stability to the state of Pakistan. This was reminiscent of Changez [Genghis] Khan, the Mongol invader known in history for his brutality, as he cut a swathe of sword and fire, leaving destruction and terror in his wake. For a while, the country seemed to be completely in Bhutto's grip. The Judiciary was tamed into obedience, the hitherto powerful Civil Service was being vigorously decimated by the insidious Lateral Entry Scheme that replaced honest, competent officers with party hacks. 'God willing and Waqar living, I will finish this bloody CSP' was an oft-quoted Bhutto war cry. Extending his aggression to wider fields, he nationalized industries, banks, and even education, so that Pakistan became unrecognizable from the state that had previously existed. But this roughshod approach, despite its initial successes, provoked the inevitable opposition, which grew in strength and compelled Bhutto into a systematic dismantling of many of his so-called 'reforms'. All of this has been chronicled by historians and political analysts, and calls for no space in this narrative, except to record my sense of concern and dismay as they played themselves out before my impotent gaze.

When the time approached for my next meeting with
Bhutto, the opposition had got the bit well within its teeth,
and I arrived in Islamabad to find myself, once again, in
the midst of a political crisis. I had been called from Tokyo
for consultations in connection with the Prime Minister's
forthcoming visit to Japan, scheduled for September, but
the prevailing atmosphere in Islamabad raised doubts in my
mind about its possibility. We had all the preparatory work
complete, and all that was necessary was for me to meet
the Prime Minister and get his final instructions. But the
outfall of the reaction to the rigging of the recent elections
was now increasing, both in terms of public outrage as well
as fury, and it was clear to me that Bhutto was going to
be too preoccupied with domestic problems to have time
for me. As I stayed on in Islamabad, cooling my heels
and waiting for an appointment with the Prime Minister,
I recalled the wise observation of the famous British
politician and historian Lord Macaulay: 'A statesman ought
to pay assiduous worship to Nemesis, to be apprehensive of
ruin when he is at the height of power and popularity, and
to dread his enemy most when most completely prostrated.'

My enforced stay in Islamabad enabled me to follow events
on the TV, supplemented with reports from friends, as
Bhutto entered into a series of tortuous negotiations with
the opposition leaders. In the process of appeasement, he
made a number of concessions to the religious parties,
starting with the declaration of Friday as the weekly holiday,
and going on to the imposition of prohibition on alcohol
all over the country (both measures were later erroneously

attributed to Zia ul-Haq). But most egregious of all was Bhutto's parliamentary legislation in 1974, declaring the Ahmadis/Qadianis a minority. That glaring piece of discriminatory legislation, an incriminating indictment, is still retained on the statute books of Pakistan.

In fact, as I cast my mind back over time, I am compelled to conclude that the origins of most acts of political evil, chicanery, and moral turpitude that currently exist, in Pakistan can be irrefutably linked to Zulfikar Ali Bhutto. The man soiled whatever he touched.

In the tense and bitter atmosphere that prevailed at the time, one could clearly sense the predicament of the cornered prime minister. Each concession that he made seemed only to whet the appetite and increase the demands of his tormentors. I was reminded of the old Russian painting which depicts, in starkly dramatic fashion, a terrified man riding through a snowstorm-covered forest in an open sleigh, desperately trying to save himself by throwing his cherished provisions, one by one, to the pack of fierce wolves howling behind in unceasing pursuit.

My prolonged stay in Islamabad was brought to an end on 3 July 1977, when I was instructed to return and seek from the Japanese government a *sine die* postponement of the prime ministerial visit. On 4 July 1977, whilst in Karachi en route to Tokyo, my orders were amended and I was instructed to remain to my post as Ambassador. Martial Law had been declared, my new boss was a largely unknown general whom I had never met, and whose name

I had hardly heard. But all that was due to change soon and substantively. For the moment, all I could see was the denouement of yet another Greek tragedy looming over Pakistan: Bhutto already had a comfortable majority in the assembly, and had no need to rig the elections.

Bhutto had been taken into detention, together with other political leaders, and as my probable meeting was now obviously cancelled, I was never to see him again. I followed, as closely as I could, his brief, stormy period of freedom, followed by his travails through the courts and the high drama that attended it, as was usual with all his public activities. Then came the agonizing months of waiting for the verdict, and the petitions, both on judicial and public interest grounds, but I discerned an ominous undertone in the observations that emanated from the Lahore High Court Bench: 'A person who considers the Constitution and the law as the handmaid of his polity is neither qualified to be elected to the high office of the Prime Minister nor can he be true to his oath'. The trial that ensued on the charges that Bhutto had ordered the assassination of a political opponent was followed worldwide and has been the subject of much scrutiny and debate, both then and since. Following the verdict of the Lahore High Court on 19 March 1978, which declared Bhutto 'the arch culprit', and pronounced the death sentence, there was a frantic effort to secure his freedom. This lasted for over a year until the Supreme Court rejected the final appeal, and Bhutto was executed at Rawalpindi Jail on 4 April 1979.

When this happened, I was at the United Nations in Geneva, and steeled myself to receive a flurry of protests, both formal and informal. But to my surprise, the reaction was only one of a strangely muted disapproval. Was this because there was no visible public outcry in Pakistan immediately following the execution? How much of this was due to the threat of brutal and efficient forces of suppression ominously poised for use, and how much was due to other causes? Whatever the reasons, the death of Bhutto left the political climate at the United Nations quite undisturbed and as placid as the waters of Lake Geneva on a summer's day. Bhutto had moved out of the delegates' horizon as they had other matters, important or trivial, to attend to.

Shortly thereafter, when I was Ambassador in France, I met Robert Badinter, the French Law Minister, who had been a great friend of Bhutto's. He was very helpful in providing residency privileges to Bhutto's family. Badinter told me that he had personally attended Bhutto's trial, and deeply regretted that much as he had wished to speak in Bhutto's defence, he was informed that a recently enacted legislation excluded foreign counsel from participation in Pakistani courts. We both pondered on the irony of fate as I gently informed Badinter that this piece of exclusivity had been legislated by Bhutto himself: he had done it to safeguard the many illegal detentions carried out by his regime.

Zulfikar Ali Bhutto is one of the two Pakistan leaders—the other being Zia ul-Haq—whose impact on the nation, for good or for evil, has been both profound and everlasting.

Bhutto took the nation with him on his wild, meteoric ride through time and space, bringing it universal honour and recognition, as during the time that he hosted the Islamic Summit; yet on frequent other occasions caring little for the damage and destruction that he caused in the reckless pursuit of his constant outrages. Above all, these egoistic orgies legitimized amorality and encouraged the spread of its venomous concept throughout society. Of course, this in due time extracted its grim price. After Bhutto, Pakistan was never the same, and whilst few if any of his achievements are worthy of note or real pride (notwithstanding the many garish monuments, memorials, and institutions sycophantically established in his name), the country is littered with the consequences of his disastrous actions and policies.

The final of these acts of *folie de grandeur*, and the one that proved fatal, was his decision to hold General Elections in 1977 and then to rig them so flagrantly. He got himself and his three Chief Ministers elected unopposed. The idea was proposed by one of his favourite bureaucrats, whom Bhutto had posted in Larkana in order to keep his opponents in line. The Chef Secretaries of the other provinces followed the example and ensured that their own Chief Ministers were re-elected unopposed, thus unintentionally ensuring that the elections lost all credibility. The agitation that ensued gathered momentum, and the end became inevitable once army brigadiers in Lahore, led by Brigadier Niaz, resigned after their refusal to fire on their own people.

So much has been written about Bhutto, both in terms of hagiography and abhorrence, that all I can do is to add a few short personal observations.

We knew each other over an intermittent period of about fifteen years, during which time we became friends, without getting too close (I was much closer to some members of his family and some of his friends.) I found our relationship to be tempered with some caution; we never really trusted each other, and I was never sure if and when he would turn on me in one of his fits of temper and public humiliation. He never did publically humiliate me; his worst with me was his cold courteousness. At work, he was arrogant, sharp, perceptive, devoid of all principle, quick to take a point as well as offence, and bore long-term grudges. He was notorious for the malicious delight that he took in elevating a person, frequently a friend, to high office, and following it with a humiliating dismissal. A brilliant negotiator, he was helped by a phenomenal memory and a chameleon ability to switch his behaviour from a browbeating bully to a cowering victim. Added to this was a sharp, pungent sense of humour. Yet this galaxy of talent could not assure him a successful outcome in his most important endeavour, that of saving his life.

He possessed an extensive library, of which he was very proud (particularly, his collection focused on Napoleon Bonaparte), and although it was touted as evidence of his wide literary talent, I always felt, when entering its premises, that its possessor had devoted more thought and attention to furnishings than content. Nevertheless, as far as politics and history are concerned, at the risk of setting the bar a bit low, it could be said that Bhutto was perhaps one of the best-read of our leaders.

In the final analysis, Zulfikar Ali Bhutto stands as one of the most memorable of Pakistan's leaders, principally because his actions and policies have done the most damage to Pakistan: from involving the country in disastrous foreign wars to an almost total destruction of the social and economic fabric of the country, and worst of all, the insidious corrosion of moral public values and mores. As I observed Bhutto over the years, ferociously clawing his own way up the political ladders and consigning to the snakes friends and foes alike, I recalled Karl Marx's observation, 'Men make their own history, but they do not make it as they please'.

Bhutto has often been called an 'evil genius', a description that whilst generally true, is rendered more accurate if the emphasis is on the adjective rather than the noun. The malign element that pervaded his character motivated many of his policies, and the consequences of these can be found in the destruction and bitterness felt in the Pakistan of today. The three factors that stood in the way of Bhutto's insatiable lust for domination and personal power were the Bengali majority, the army, and many Baloch Sardars whom Bhutto had alienated. He drove the country into two wars and a messy breakup of Pakistan. This was the legacy that Zulfikar Ali Bhutto left behind.

Distrust all men in whom the urge to punish is powerful.

Friedrich Nietzsche

NOTES

1. *Zulfi Bhutto of Pakistan: His Life and Times* by Stanley Wolpert (Oxford University Press, 1993).
2. *Zulfi Bhutto of Pakistan: His Life and Times* by Stanley Wolpert (Oxford University Press, 1993); *If I Am Assassinated* by Zulfikar Ali Bhutto (Tarang Paperbacks, 1982); *Zulfiqar Ali Bhutto of Pakistan, Last Days* by Kauṣar Niyāzī (Vikas Pub. House, 1992).
3. See, *Quiet Diplomacy: Memoirs of an Ambassador of Pakistan* (Karachi: Oxford University Press, 2010).
4. Ibid.
5. Ibid.

7

General Mohammad Zia ul-Haq:
1977–1988

Nicht durch Reden oder Majoritätsbeschlüsse
warden die großen Fragen der Zeit entschieden ...
sondern durch Eisen und Blut.

(The great questions of the time will be determined not by
speeches or majority decisions ... but by iron and blood)

Otto von Bismarck

As I waited in Karachi for my airline connection to Tokyo, where I was instructed to return, there appeared before my mind's eye a disturbing déjà vu: the recollection of the breakdown of political negotiations, followed by the disruption of civil order, followed by a military takeover. Zia ul-Haq's broadcast, which I had listened to the previous night, ended on what was then a seemingly reassuring note: 'Pakistan, which was created in the name of Islam, will continue to survive only if it sticks to Islam. That is why I consider the introduction of an Islamic system as an essential prerequisite for the country'. In the event, Zia would free us from the shackles of Bhutto's spurious socialism, but at a cost that would impose its own harsh terms.

However, whilst sitting in the departure lounge at the Karachi Airport on the hot summer morning of 1 July 1977, I could never have imagined that this was the start of a political regime that would last a decade, and would usher a transformation in Pakistan that would be both fundamental and indelible. Bhutto and Zia were the two men who, each in their individual fashion, had inflicted upon Pakistan widely different forms of government, radically opposite in both concept and implementation; the only common feature between the two was the lasting impact that each cast upon the country.

My first meeting with General Zia ul-Haq took place during the early period of transition when, with Zulfikar Ali Bhutto and the other political leaders in detention, the Chief Martial Law Administrator (CMLA), as Zia was now known, was casting about for his next move. I was received late in the evening in the drawing room of the Army House. It was a simply furnished middle-class residence that underwent little change of appearance over the next ten years. I was escorted by Foreign Secretary Shah Nawaz, and Zia ul-Haq rose to give us a very friendly greeting as we entered the room. The heavy, dark moustache and hooded eyelids made a somewhat sinister initial impression, but behind the thick eyeglasses there sparkled a pair of bright brown eyes filled with intelligence and affecting a quiet attractive warmth. Although clad in uniform, his body language was totally devoid of swagger, and seemed to suggest an innate modesty. This was somewhat in contrast to the public image of a roughshod, newly arrived military dictator. Our conversation was pleasant, rather than profound, and after a short while, as I took leave with Zia wishing me success in my mission, I thought that it should be an interesting experience to work under a decisive man who possessed powerful convictions, and yet was not entirely free of contradictions.

My next meeting with Zia ul-Haq was when I joined the Pakistan delegation, led by him as President, to the Conference of Heads of State and Government of the Non-Aligned Nations, held at Havana, Cuba. Since this was the first time that Pakistan had participated as a member of the group, it was an important meeting, both in substance and symbol. It was also probably the first time that Zia had led a Pakistan delegation to an international conference, and I was impressed by the enthusiasm with which he followed the briefings and reports presented to him by members of the high-powered delegation that accompanied him. There were some tendentious issues, which Zia appeared to have taken in his stride. Two amongst these were the Cuban Draft Resolution declaring the Soviet Union as 'the natural ally of the Non-Aligned Movement'; and another draft, sponsored by the radical Arab states, calling for the expulsion of Egypt from the Non-Aligned Movement following the Camp David Accord. Zia perused the briefs assiduously, discussed the issues with us, and arrived at pragmatic conclusions. The result was that, in its first appearance at a Non-Aligned Conference, the Pakistan delegation made a positive contribution. But as we worked with near-cheerful optimism in Havana, some disturbing items of news kept filtering in from Pakistan; perhaps the most egregious and damaging being the reports, accompanied by photographs, of public floggings carried out in the presence of disgustingly appreciative crowds. It was a chilling foretaste of events to come during the Zia administration. Almost as vivid, but much less barbaric, was the change in the sartorial composition of the Pakistan delegation: those who came from Islamabad were dressed in crisp white *achkans*, whereas those of us who came from other capitals, where subtle pressures to adapt the new dress code had not yet reached, were in western garb.

Also, at Zia's unabashed request, I was obliged to listen to him as he rehearsed his major speeches, and check them less for their content than to correct, in Zia's words, 'my Punjabi English pronunciation'. But Zia dispensed with this precaution in a very short time. He was a quick learner, had entered into his new role as Head of Government with a rapid, self assured élan, and relished the exercise of power. Also, he consistently exercised the utmost courtesy in his dealings with the members of all delegations, and especially his own. It was hard to imagine that a man who was so effectively spreading sweetness and light abroad was simultaneously heading an administration with such a barbaric domestic record. It was during our early association in Havana that I was first struck by this dichotomy in Zia ul-Haq's character, and it remained with me, unresolved, from Cuba until his plane crash in the Bahawalpur desert in August 1988.

The coup of July 1977, which had removed Bhutto from office, presented Zia with a twofold dilemma. The first was that Bhutto still retained a considerable degree of popular support, as was evident from the substantial attendance at his public meetings. The second issue was the legitimacy of Zia's action, highlighted by a suit filed by Begum Nusrat Bhutto which challenged the validity of the imposed Martial Law and accused Zia of treason by violating Article 6 of the 1973 Constitution. It may be mentioned here, that according to a widely circulated account of the events of those times, Zia called on Z. A. Bhutto at the place of the latter's incarceration in Murree and was arrogantly greeted with the grim query, 'General, have you read Article 6 of the Constitution?' If this was true, then the battle lines appear to have been drawn quite early. Of course, I was not present at this meeting, but I do recall seeing in the newspapers of the time a vivid photograph of that encounter; it depicts Zia in full uniform, somewhat apprehensively perched on the edge of his chair, and Bhutto in an immaculate lounge suit, looking equally tense, with eyes glowering and lips tightly pursed.

It was at this time that all Pakistani Heads of Mission received a somewhat peremptory circular letter, marked 'SECRET' and signed by Foreign Secretary Sultan Khan, indicating the determination of the new regime to remain in office, induct its policies, and its expectation of compliance, in letter and spirit, by all ambassadors. We all knew that this warning shot across our bows came from the office of the CMLA (Chief Martial Law Administrator), and not from the Foreign Office; neither was it a mere pro forma bureaucratic exercise. In any case, I had never before or since, in my long diplomatic career, seen a missive bearing implications of such dire consequences.

After the *coup*, Zia ul-Haq dealt with the first of the two problems that confronted him: the publicly demonstrated popularity of Bhutto. He arrested Bhutto and then activated an FIR (First Information Report) against him for murder originally filed in 1974 by Ahmad Raza Kasuri, at a time when Bhutto was Prime Minister and Kasuri was a maverick member of Bhutto's Pakistan Peoples Party (PPP). The second problem, the issue of legitimacy, was deftly dealt with by Zia ul-Haq and his legal adviser, Syed Sharifuddin Pirzada, a brilliant lawyer known for his dexterous abilities in the field of constitutional law. They invoked a 1954 decision of the Supreme Court whereby the concept of 'The Doctrine of Necessity' was propounded as justification for the dismissal of the National Assembly by Governor General Ghulam Mohammed. This was, therefore, conveniently used as a precedent for a similar decision by the Supreme Court in November 1977 to justify the imposition of Martial Law by Zia ul-Haq. The stark reality of military rule, which the country had now come to accept in any case, and had in fact been welcomed by those who were opposed to Bhutto's idiosyncratic fascist tendencies, had thus been granted a legal status, and this landmark decision was now beyond challenge. Zia had succeeded in covering his military iron fist with a velvet glove provided to him by the Supreme Court.

The actions initiated by Zia in 1977 were in consonance with the views that he had expressed when he staged the *coup d'état*, that 'an Islamic system is an essential prerequisite for the country', and proved that his words were not mere expressions, and that he meant what he had said. Every time that I visited Pakistan during the period immediately following Zia's coup, I was able to observe these changes and the manner in which they were being implemented. In all government offices, there were statutory provisions for the allocation of time and space for daily prayers, which heads of departments were encouraged to lead. The dress code of the bureaucracy had changed, almost overnight, from ties and three-piece suits to *achkans*, *shalwars*, and waistcoats. Also, there was a disgusting increase in the hypocritical public display of piety, which had by now become a major component of the insidious cult of the obsequious that has always plagued our society.

In his personal conduct and deportment, Zia always remained polite and low-key. He was no Savonarola, breathing fire and brimstone in the cause of religion. I often heard him say, 'What is between you and God is your personal affair, and has nothing to do with me or anybody else'. But in the domain of public policy, his devotion to Islam was meaningful and unequivocal. During my intermittent visits to Pakistan, I was able to observe the manner in which Zia was increasing his hold over the country, and what I saw was not entirely comforting. He postponed elections in 1977 as well as in 1979. He referred to this in a personal conversation some years later, when we had got to know each other quite well. He wryly admitted, 'I know I do not have a very good track record as far as elections are concerned.'

Furthermore, Zia's introduction and implementation of a series of draconian Martial Law regulations and punishments, including the barbaric system of public floggings, was perhaps the biggest black mark against his regime. For public humiliation and national shame, it remains unsurpassed in the history of the twentieth century, and a claim against which we had no defence when conducting our international diplomacy. The official line provided to us—that the government was implementing a law on our statute books dating from British colonial days—was as derisory as were references to the limitations on methods of flogging as 'prescribed under Islamic law'. Fortunately for us, one element that helped us in the short term was the decrease in the number of repulsive sentences imposed and executed under the outrageous Martial Law Regulations. On the other hand, Zulfikar Ali Bhutto's fate remained a matter of great public concern throughout 1978 and the early months of 1979. The dramatic proceedings in the Lahore High Court, and later in the Supreme Court, were followed within the nation and abroad with the greatest interest. My own impression at that time, confirmed in retrospective consideration, was that Bhutto's arrogance, coupled with the manifest incompetence of his counsel Yahya Bakhtiar, had between them, thoroughly bungled the case for Bhutto's defence. For his part, Zia ul-Haq went through the gamut of the formalities of the entire legal process in his cool and methodical manner. Following the unanimous death sentence pronounced by the Lahore High Court in March 1978, the case was heard in appeal by the Supreme Court. Of the nine-member bench, one retired during the course of the hearing and another withdrew because of illness. A split decision, with three judges siding with Chief Justice Anwar ul-Haq, confirmed the sentence passed by the Lahore High Court. In conformity with statutory requirements, a mercy petition was submitted and rejected, by the Ministerial Cabinet, the Punjab Governor, and the Martial Law Administrative Council respectively. Messages from several world leaders urging clemency were ignored. In an interview with Gavin Young of the London Observer on 1 October 1978, Zia had said, 'If the Supreme Court says "Acquit him", I will acquit him. If it says, "Hang the blighter", I will hang him'. On 4 April 1979, Zia proved true to his grim promise.

Some years later, after Zia and I had got to know each other quite well, I was invited to attend, the informal brainstorming sessions that he convened. After the meeting in the drawing room of the Army House was over and most of the participants had departed, a few of us would stay on and chat late into the night. It was on one of these occasions that Zia, looking pensive, troubled, and thoughtful, his eyes gazing into space and ignoring everyone in the room, lowered his voice and said something that none of us could quite hear. The gist appeared to be that, during one of his visits to Mecca, Zia had sought divine guidance and support for how he should deal with Bhutto; after that, all was clear. This extraordinary mumbled recollection remained in my troubled memory for many years: was it a genuine mea culpa, or the customary masterful casuistry? What provoked the thought, and what exactly did he say? Was Zia really convinced that he had received a divine preordained sanction to execute Bhutto? Or was this Bismarck's 'sondern durch Eisen und Blut' (but by iron and blood)?

Zia's working hours began quite late in the day, with most of the time spent in his office at the Army House, which was also the venue for most Cabinet Meetings. It became apparent that Zia had, early in his tenure, firmly established his authority and gone on to exercise it in increasingly ruthless fashion. Although he conducted his meetings and conferences with confidence, he remained a low key, almost silent participant, who kept his thoughts very much to himself. It was almost impossible, for me at any rate, to draw any definitive conclusions of what he was thinking. Also, he was extremely cool under fire, and could not be provoked into outbursts of anger, except when he deliberately chose to do so as a negotiating tactic. Many of his rivals have turned into victims through their failure to realize his mastery over the old ploy of 'don't get mad, get even'.

As already mentioned, Zia carried out his demanding functions as Head of State and Chief of Army Staff during normal daylight working hours from the Aiwan-e-Sadr (President's House), a modern, Edward Stone designed edifice which provoked Zia's contempt for not being sufficiently 'Islamic', i.e. lacking domes and minarets. But his substantial work was done, and important decisions were taken at the GHQ (General Headquarters), where there was naturally no civilian participation. Almost equally significant were the informal late-night sessions at the Army House, where the usual participants were General Arif, Agha Shahi, Sahabzada Yaqub Khan, Ghulam Ishaq Khan, Generals Ghulam Jilani and Akhtar Abdul Rehman, Sardar Shah Nawaz, and a couple of senior officials whose names I cannot now recollect. I was sometimes invited to attend these meetings, where the main topics of discussion were usually Afghanistan and the nuclear issue. It was fascinating to observe the cool, steely resolve which the President and Ghulam Ishaq brought to bear in dealing with these issues which were, of course, the most vital that confronted Pakistan at that period.

Although I had several meetings with Zia over the course of time, both individually and in committees, I emerged from most without being quite sure of his underlying motivations and intentions: he possessed a masterly instinct for playing things close to his chest. The manner in which Zia staged his coup and the smoothness of the assumption of power are a matter of historic record. This includes the Delphic warning that he issued to Bhutto at the height of the agitation: 'If the agitation does not end, it can erode the army's discipline, and cause divisions within the ranks'. I was in Islamabad during those eventful days, but knew nothing about the details of the tense negotiations that pervaded the halls of power. Apart from sensing the aura of high drama that pervaded the atmosphere of the time, we in the public got to know very little of what was really going on. We were informed only of the composition of the Military Council, and its assurance that elections would be held within ninety days. Based upon this constitutionally dubious, but unassailably realistic assumption, Zia went about the consolidation of his powers, a phenomenon that became increasingly evident on each of my successive visits to the country. Equally notable and disturbing was the docile public acceptance of this process of denigration of freedoms.

After a while, I came to the conclusion that, with the clear and obvious exception of Muhammad Ali Jinnah, no leader in Pakistan had his hands as firmly on the levers of power as Zia ul-Haq. The latter's administration reflected his character: efficient, determined, bold, and ruthless. He was the first Pakistan Army Chief without a Sandhurst or Indian Military Academy qualification, and emerged from a solid, conservative middle-class background. This made him ideally suited to understand the thinking and mores of the troops and junior officers. Later, this valuable asset was extended to his deft handling of political affairs nationwide. He had the ability to concern himself with every aspect of the country's affairs, ranging from the mundane district administration to the conduct of national policies, and his firm hand set the country surely and purposefully on the Islamic track. Nevertheless, Zia in his individual attitude never turned his back on knowledge and progress, and after we had got to know each other well, I was assigned the pleasant duty of selecting and sending him any books that I thought might be of interest to him. During the course of this exercise, which lasted several months, I found that Zia not only read most of the books that had been sent to him but discussed them with relish, particularly the more provocative volumes. Even though I profoundly disagreed with many of his views and his actions, and expressed my opposition to them quite frankly, my remonstrations were met with nothing but silence and a deep stare from those dark, hooded eyes. It was during this period that I became aware of Zia's political courage and coolness under fire. He stood up to the Russians over Afghanistan, and stood up to the Americans on the issue of the administration of resources received in support of the Afghan resistance. And on the volatile issue of the nuclear programme, Zia and Ghulam Ishaq Khan, stood up against the entire world with cool courage.

It was not till much later, when I had become privy to some of the thinking of the ruling political elite, that I noticed the only hint of fear in Zia's mind. It took the shape of a cautionary plea to his friend General Faiz Ali Chishti, who was affectionately referred to by Zia as *'Murshid'* (mentor, guide), and who was charged with the implementation of 'Operation Fairplay', the code name for the coup. Zia had said to Chishti: *'Murshid, mujhai mat marwa dena'* (*Murshid*, don't get me killed).

Zia survived that crisis and went on to take Pakistan into the nuclear age.

But in 1978, Zia was very far from that position. The military coup and the harsh, repressive measures that followed had, quite rightly and not unexpectedly, placed us in an indefensible position, and not one from which it was possible to conduct diplomacy with any comfort. Conditions remained in this state of limbo until December 1979, when the Soviet invasion of Afghanistan presented the world with a fait accompli which overturned the carefully nurtured international détente following the Helsinki Accords. All over the world, chanceries began to review and reassess their position in an international environment that threatened a menacing change. The vagaries of world affairs were about to transform Pakistan from an international pariah into an international poster boy. The man who saw this, and trimmed his sails to catch the winds of opportunity for his country, was General Zia ul-Haq.

In Washington, an initial muddled and pusillanimous response by President Jimmy Carter underwent a radical change, thanks to the Chief of his National Security Agency, Zbigniew Brzezinski, who asserted his authority and his expertise on the USSR to assemble a credible resistance to the Soviet action, to increase diplomatic cooperation with Pakistan and to provide it with economic and military assistance. Delegations from western capitals began to drop into Islamabad like rotten fruit, and Zia ul-Haq assembled a very competent team of high-level advisers who, in turn, devised a most effective routine of receptions, briefings, and hospitality that sent the visitors back home happy and charged with fervour for the cause. My post in Geneva required close and continuous participation in these activities, including frequent visits to Islamabad and consultations with officials, ministers, and the president which brought me a bit nearer to the decision-makers and the centres of power (I felt as though I had been temporarily moved from cover point to second slip), and this in turn gave me an opportunity to observe at closer quarters the workings of the administration and of Zia ul-Haq himself. It was also during this period that Arnaz and I developed a family friendship with the President and Begum Zia, who grew particularly fond of Arnaz, whose many virtues, in Begum Zia's estimation, included Arnaz's resemblance to her favourite Indian film star, Nargis. We were impressed by the simplicity of their lifestyle, and touched by the care and devotion which they bestowed upon their daughter who was a special child.

Shortly after taking office, Zia ul-Haq displayed an act of bold and imaginative statesmanship which, unfortunately, has not been either recognized or remembered these days. A bitter and bloody insurgency in Balochistan had commenced immediately after Bhutto had dismissed the duly-elected government and imprisoned the Baloch leaders, including Ghaus Bux Bizenjo, Ataullah Mengal, and a number of others. A ruthless campaign had been carried out by the army under Tikka Khan against the Baloch people, with widespread casualties on both sides. Overcoming the objections of his senior generals (in itself an act of courage during the early period of his regime), Zia called off the military action and entered into negotiations with the Baloch leaders. Meeting them in person and in prison, Zia ordered their release, proclaimed them free and loyal citizens of Pakistan, and ordered the recall of troops to their peacetime stations. He did all this as he sat on the floor and had lunch with the Baloch leaders at their place of detention in the Hyderabad jail. He also arranged for Ataullah Mengal to go abroad for medical treatment at government's expense. After that lunch on the prison floor, Balochistan returned to peace, and Zia never had a problem with the province for the next eight years of his regime.

It was obvious that Afghanistan, a crisis of international dimensions, was occupying most of Zia's time and attention. I was no expert on the domestic political issues in Pakistan, but it was clear to me that they were by no means settled and required constant supervision. Although never averse to the use of cruel and ruthless measures, once he had established his hold on the political system, Zia mainly exercised power through his superb organizational capability. Of all the presidents with whom I have had the privilege to work, none had his hands more firmly on the administration. Also, coming from a pious and industrious middle-class background, Zia seemed, particularly during the early period of his rule, to have had quite an uncanny sense of the thoughts and feelings of the common man. His personal piety remains unquestioned, but observations during my repeated visits to Pakistan gradually convinced me that his emphasis on religion was a political tool that he was manipulating with some cynicism and much success.

Whilst this enabled him to achieve his immediate objective of remaining in power, its long-term consequences on the country were profoundly and disastrously reactionary.

Despite his external and internal preoccupations, Zia did not let his sight waver from his other major objective. It became clear to me that, with the close cooperation of patriots like Ghulam Ishaq Khan, Zia was pursuing the nuclear programme with stealth and determination. The policy with India was also a most interesting study. Like all good generals, Zia did not believe in fighting on several fronts at the same time. Without being in any way effusive, he kept relations with New Delhi on an even keel, eschewed provocative pronouncements, and thus discreetly shifted Kashmir to the back-burner. As a sideline, he refurbished the Sikh shrines in Pakistan and encouraged pilgrimages, leaving me with the agreeable suspicion that Zia had a soft spot for the Sikhs.

My visits to Islamabad, as already stated, had increased in frequency, involving not only conferences and meetings with visiting delegations, but also occasional restricted consultations with the president and foreign minister. These latter meetings were mostly late-night sessions at the Army House, and provided me with a close exposure to Zia's methods of work. Always cool and composed, he was both a good listener and a quick learner, never taking offence, regardless of the outrageous nature of the provocation. The meetings were conducted in a civilized manner, and a frank and candid exchange of views was encouraged, with Zia acting as conciliator when necessary. With Ghulam Ishaq a frequent participant, one could be sure that the talks were focused. Although I frequently left that drawing room with uncomfortable feelings of concern about the lack of any liberal element in the discussions that had just taken place, there was complete certainty in my mind that there were strong hands at the helm of affairs. And always, there was President Zia ul-Haq to walk you to the door, shake your hands warmly, see you into your car, and give you his farewell smile and bow as you were driven away.

In my view, one of Zia ul-Haq's greatest achievements was his key role in the creation, against a series of almost impossible odds, of Pakistan's nuclear capability. As far back as 1956, Pakistan had established the Pakistan Atomic Energy Commission (PAEC), which basically concentrated on fundamental research, particularly high-energy physics. But the greatest benefit accrued to Pakistan at this period was through the foresight and initiative of one of PAEC's early Directors, Dr Ishrat Husain Usmani, a CSP (Civil Service of Pakistan) officer endowed with dynamism and egoism in equal measure who took full advantage of the talent available in the country and established a cadre of scientists through an extensive provision and distribution of scholarships, both domestic and international. Thus in due course, we had our own reserves of talent, ranging from nuclear physicists, to metallurgists, to chemical engineers, to plumbers—the entire expertise that is necessary to create and maintain a sophisticated nuclear programme.

However, the true political quest for the nuclear grail had commenced with Zulfikar Ali Bhutto. In early 1972, he called all the known nuclear scientists of Pakistan, including future Nobel Laureate Professor Abdus Salam, to a covert meeting in Multan. Here he stressed the importance of Pakistan's acquisition of nuclear capability in order to secure its safety and prestige, and exhorted them to produce a nuclear bomb. The response was an enthusiastic and spontaneous roar of approval and an assurance by the scientists that they could do it. After that, they began to work, but progress was hampered by the usual Pakistani impediments of intrigue and lethargy, until the arrival of A. Q. Khan, whose presence and flair for personal publicity created a new plateau for the nuclear issue. In due course, following the departure of Bhutto, the subject came under the tight control and supervision of Zia ul-Haq, in close collaboration with Ghulam Ishaq Khan. It was the foresight, determination, and political skill of these two dedicated patriots that manoeuvred the (still formally unacknowledged) entry of Pakistan into the group of nuclear weapon states. The story of Pakistan's nuclear quest has been recorded by many writers, observers, and self-styled 'experts', most of whom are accusatory and alarmist; others, less numerous, are self-promotional and boastful.

My association with the nuclear project commenced at the time of my posting to Bonn, and thereafter retained peripheral status. It was also restrained by the constraints of secrecy. The Embassy had a Procurement Department (the nomenclature really fooled nobody) headed by a most able officer of minister rank named Ikram Khan, who was seconded from our nuclear establishment headed by

Dr A. Q. Khan. Ikram was a superb officer, knowledgeable, low-key and efficient, and went about his sensitive job with the combination of initiative and discretion that were its primary requirements. This was the era when Pakistan's nuclear programme was under the strictest international surveillance, and we had the greatest difficulty both in procurement for the project as well as concealment of its development. The understanding on which I operated was, firstly, to have direct access to the President. The next was to ensure the security of the procurement process and guard against any scam or entrapment; matters of pricing or technical capabilities of the equipment obtained were excluded from my supervision. This exercise involved a bit of James Bond stuff, and I remember Ikram and myself meeting characters, genuine and shady, in tiny cafes tucked away in obscure villages deep in the beautiful Swiss and German countryside. There I sipped the excellent local wines, and Ikram the local apple and other fruit juices, whilst we assessed and evaluated the items on offer. The constraints of security prevent further disclosure, but I remember being astonished at the nature and quantum of the items that Ikram was able to ferret out. His low-key, reassuring approach, and quiet but extensive contacts had established a reputation for integrity and reliability in the foggy and mysterious market of nuclear suppliers. It is not possible to reveal anything further, other than stating that our delicate task was to make the right choices.

On my transfer from Bonn to Paris, I was instructed to continue my association with the Procurement Department and report to the President. On recalling this period, I remain in admiration of the manner in which it was handled overall, first by Zia ul-Haq and then by Ghulam Ishaq Khan. I maintain a mild, amused contempt for the enthusiasm with which western industrial enterprises, in their pecuniary pursuits, conspired with us to evade their own governments' law prohibiting all nuclear transfers to Pakistan.

Meanwhile, Zia continued his blatant lie in denying that Pakistan was seeking nuclear weapons. He did this despite three Pakistan-specific Congressional Amendments (Symington, Glenn, Solarz) that imposed penalties for infraction, and also despite numerous personal meetings with high-level American representatives from the Congress and the Administration urging restraint on nuclear proliferation. Confronting the threats from the Americans at that period was a remarkable act of courage and patriotism, and one which is unfortunately not recognized these days.

As the Zia ul-Haq regime continued, it was evident that there had been a noticeable resurgence on the economic front. Thanks largely to prudent management by a disciplined bureaucracy under Ghulam Ishaq Khan, and the timely infusion of US and foreign assistance which had been provided for the Afghan war, the country was in apparent stability. But despite the seemingly reassuring factors of national economic progress and peace, Zia, like all usurpers of power before and after him, faced the problem of legitimacy, and sought a solution through his own brand of sleight of hand. I know that this was agitating his mind. Each time that I met him on my visits home, he would mention it indirectly during our informal talks, as would his principal adviser General Arif. I could see that the years of Zia's grim repressive regime had begun to take its toll on the people, and Pakistan was beginning to become a resentful soulless society. Zia's response to this situation was at first uncharacteristically tentative, and then equally uncharacteristically brash. He first set up a nominated Advisory Council, appropriately named *Majlis-e-Shura*, and when that failed to click, he resorted to a referendum, a time-worn device of all dictators: not unexpectedly, the loaded question could produce only one answer and one result.

All I became aware of was that under the new Constitution, a party-less assembly confirmed Muhammad Khan Junejo as Prime Minister, with full executive powers, whilst the only powers that Zia ul-Haq as President possessed was to dismiss the Prime Minister and the assembly, and then call for elections. I was astonished at this arrangement because, as I saw it (in terms of the nuclear jargon with which we were familiar at the time), this meant in effect, that Junejo was provided with conventional weapons, which he could deploy from time to time, whereas Zia could only exercise his nuclear option once. I must admit that I did not express these apprehensions to Zia even once during the frequent meetings that we had during those days. Why didn't I? The unsatisfactory answer is partly because it was none of my business, and 'well above my pay grade', and partly because I was according priority to working on two other problems: (a) those concerned with the implementation of the Geneva Accords; and (b) the nuclear issue and the threat of sanctions. Above all, there were the overriding demands of the regime change associated with the unusual manner of the appointment of Muhammad Khan Junejo as Prime Minister of Pakistan. Later on, when I discussed this matter with Roedad Khan, he told me that he had, in fact, brought up the subject in a Cabinet Meeting, pointing out that under the rules of business, the Prime Minister would be the deciding authority on all matters, and not the President. Zia's response was that he would be able to 'control everything from above.'

Men commit the error of not knowing when to limit their hopes.

Machiavelli, Discourses

8

Muhammad Khan Junejo: 1985–1988

THE MOUSE THAT ROARED

Muhammad Khan Junejo was Prime Minister of Pakistan from 1985–1988. He was an agriculturist from Sindh who, like many of his kind, had been active in both provincial and national politics, wherein he had attained a modicum of success and stature. His elevation to the post of Prime Minister of Pakistan was less due to any innate capability than to a combination of connections, circumstances, and the good fortune that is the quintessential requirement of success in politics. Junejo had been a true and faithful member of the Muslim League, and was also a follower (mureed) of the Pir Pagara, one of the most influential landowners and religious leaders in Sindh. It was believed that Zia had appointed Junejo as Prime Minister largely at the behest of Pir Pagara, who possesses considerable political clout in the province.

HONEST, INCORRUPTIBLE; LACKING POLITICAL SKILL, COMPREHENSION, INITIATIVE

Until he became Prime Minister, my acquaintance with Junejo was slight and largely social. I had regarded him as a pleasant Sindhi Zamindar who was not too informed but was always courteous and helpful. This impression changed considerably once I got to know him and work for him. The courtesies were always there, but behind the facade of amiability there was a surprising crafty capability and stubborn determination. Above all, his personal financial integrity stood as tall and upright as the man himself.

Junejo's relationship with Zia ul-Haq started off on a rocky note and never quite assumed an even keel, which was unfortunate for both men, and especially so for Pakistan. It is reported that at their first meeting, when Zia informed Junejo that he intended to appoint him Prime Minister, the latter expressed his gratitude with the demand, 'When are you going to lift Martial Law, Mister President?' From that point, their relationship went steadily downhill.

From the beginning of my association with Junejo, it became clear to me that the Prime Minister, though neither well-read nor experienced in statecraft, nevertheless seemed to possess an instinctive crafty sense of survival. This, combined with his personal integrity and his low public profile, were the impressions that I obtained from his performance during the early days of his office, and which lasted throughout his tenure. Retiring by nature, he was conscious of his discomfort with the use of the English language, a fact which rendered him slow and awkward during international negotiations. I was told that he spent most of his off-duty leisure hours in the Prime Minister's drawing room gossiping with Sindhi Section Officers in order to keep abreast of the prevailing situation.

Early during my work with Junejo, I noticed that he was essentially an aural creature, that he read very little, and that briefs conveyed to him verbally in either English or Urdu got through to him much more quickly and effectively than those conveyed in writing. Accordingly, I adopted this approach, among others, in my dealings with Junejo and found him to be both receptive and, within the limits of his capability, effective. In due course, we developed a relationship which induced him to include me as a working member of the delegation during his official visit to Washington and Paris. This association was further developed in the informal exchange of views and that we would have over cups of tea and coffee during the free time that is inevitably included in the schedules of most state or official visits.

I found Junejo to be a receptive, if somewhat slow learner, with stubborn beliefs and views that were difficult to argue out. Highly suspicious by nature, his instinctive approach to anything new that he might encounter was one of distrust, coupled with an undisguised pettiness. For example, when I attempted the important task to brief him on the discussions that took place at a meeting between Zia ul-Haq and Ronald Reagan, so that we could prepare our own position notes on the forthcoming meeting with the US President, I discovered that Junejo's priority was for us to ensure that he would be lodged in the same hotel (and even the same suite) that had been provided to Zia ul-Haq at the earlier meeting! I must admit that melding inn-keeping with diplomacy was both difficult and unexpected. In this case, we were successful, thanks only to my wife Arnaz who, because of her previous experience and contacts as a leading hotelier, helped us to pull it off.

Junejo lost no time in exercising his powers as Prime Minister. Initially, it was on relatively innocuous political issues, such as putting government officials, including army generals, into small Suzuki cars instead of the luxurious BMWs and Mercedes that they had become accustomed to. Or else, he exerted his powers in matters of postings and transfers of civilian officials, particularly those in Sindh. He began to show his muscle in appointments to important assignments in the federal administration also. He replaced serving and retired army officers with civilians (the most notable being the high-profile Information Secretary. Lt Gen. Mujibur Rahman). Gradually, as he began to spread his ambit of power, Junejo rejected a number of Zia's nominations in delegations going on foreign missions, and extended this process of rejection to Zia's nominations for cabinet posts.

Junejo's pinpricks on Zia were turning into stabs, and the battle lines were by now clearly drawn. The most important of these differences arose over the issue of the appointment of Finance and Foreign Ministers, with the Finance portfolio very deservedly going to Mahbub ul Haq, an eminent international economist, and Zia's nominee. The appointment of the Foreign Minister was the subject of a much more serious dispute between the President and the Prime Minister, and was settled by a compromise— Sahabzada Yaqub Khan was appointed as Foreign

Minister—and Zain Noorani, a long-standing member of the Muslim League, as Deputy Foreign Minister. Like so many compromise arrangements, this was a recipe for disaster. Yaqub Khan and Noorani were poles apart in character, temperament, and disposition. Whilst Yaqub was an urbane, sophisticated Nawab, fluent in several languages and elegant in appearance; Noorani, despite his outward sartorial pretensions, was basically a street-smart Karachi politician. We all knew that Yaqub was Zia's man charged to watch Noorani; and that Noorani was Junejo's man charged to watch Yaqub. This did not render the Foreign Office a very convivial place to work in.

The favourable winds that blew Junejo into the Prime Minister's seat continued to favour him during the early part of his tenure. As the Afghanistan situation heated its way towards a conclusion, international attention on Pakistan increased in proportion, and Junejo found himself consorting with world leaders both at home and abroad. And when I say 'world leaders', I mean the likes of Ronald Reagan and Jacques Chirac. This was heady stuff. As I accompanied Junejo on many of these engagements, I could see that he was enjoying these interactions thoroughly. Even though he would be frequently out of depth, he was seldom phased, leaving it to his confused interlocutor to draw his own conclusions whilst Junejo bumbled his amiable self-satisfied way through.

Within the Foreign Ministry, however, the situation was not quite as benign, and one could sense, on an almost daily basis, a sharpening of the proxy war being fought by

Yaqub Khan and Zain Noorani on behalf of their principals
Zia ul-Haq and Junejo. Whilst a number of lesser issues
were settled at the ministerial level, the major problem, of
course, arose over the final negotiations and the signature
of the Geneva Agreement concerning the withdrawal of
troops from Afghanistan. Junejo was anxious to conclude
the negotiations as soon as possible, since they were
proceeding satisfactorily, whereas Zia tried to delay the
signature of the accords, and their implementation, until
he had sent more arms to the mujahideen, and had also
established a regime in Kabul that would be favourable to
Pakistan.

Through the smoke and speculation that was rife at that
time, there emerged two clear facts. The first was that
Junejo dismissed Sahabzada Yaqub Khan and replaced him
with Zain Noorani. The second was that the Afghanistan
talks were concluded on 10 April 1988, with the Geneva
Accords being signed on behalf of Pakistan by the new
Foreign Minister Zain Noorani; who, in his newly flushed
enthusiasm, retained the pen which he had used for the
purpose, and proudly carried it with him on his subsequent
victory lap in Karachi.

Suspicions and bitterness between Zia and Junejo continued
to escalate. It came to a point where the two were hardly
speaking to each other. For me, it was a particularly delicate
period. Not only was I on friendly terms with both, but
my increasing involvement in foreign affairs matters also
put me in closer contact with both of them. Added to this
drama was Junejo's illness—everybody except he himself

seemed to think he was dying of cancer. Under normal circumstances, Junejo was soft-spoken, but due to his illness, his voice had sunk to an almost inaudible whisper. Accompanying him at international meetings could be difficult, embarrassing, and uncomfortable.

Nevertheless, in a vivid illustration of the chaotic and bizarre political conditions that prevailed at the time, just as Junejo returned home after leading a Pakistan delegation abroad, Zia struck. On 19 May 1988, the President exercised his political 'nuclear option' and dismissed in one stroke his hand-picked Prime Minister and the nominated Parliament. The reasons provided by the administration for this move at a hastily summoned press conference the next day were 'rampant corruption, nepotism, and maladministration, finally leading to a complete breakdown of morality and law and order in the country'. Following this absurd, self-serving pronouncement, Muhammad Khan Junejo made a few muted noises and retreated to his village in Sindh 'unwept, un-honoured and unsung'.

In 1993, Muhammad Khan Junejo succumbed to his malady, the cancer that he had so bravely battled against in his final years.

9

Zia ul-Haq: May–August 1988

REDUX

I was obliged to make a number of visits to Pakistan for consultations in 1987. These were fleeting two- or three-day visits, charged with calls on the President, Prime Minister, and meetings at the Foreign Office. Each of these trips increased my concerns about the relations between the power elite of the country. Differences between the President and Prime Minister appeared to increase with the passage of time, with attitudes moving from suspicion to acrimony and finally to downright hostility. It was not a comfortable situation, and by no means conducive to the unity and understanding so essential to meet the three major foreign policy issues that confronted us. These were, as I saw them at the time: (a) our relations with Washington, where we were simultaneously dealing with the aid package and the nuclear issue; (b) the negotiations in Geneva, which were in their penultimate stage; and (c) the unexpected threat from India posed by Operation Brasstacks (1986–1987), an ominous and massive military exercise unleashed by its hawkish Army Commander General Krishnaswamy Sunderji.

I noted that Zia tackled each of these issues almost single-handedly, and met with varying degrees of success. In the case of Brasstacks, Zia took off on a private and unannounced pilgrimage to Ajmer, with an added visit to an Indo-Pakistan cricket match which was being played at that same time. Having created this opportunity, Zia utilized it to defuse tensions over Brasstacks by issuing soothing messages.

The other two issues formed the core of the brief of the unofficial negotiations conducted in Pakistan between Zia and two senior US officials, Richard Armitage, Assistant Secretary for International Security in the Department of Defence, and Richard Murphy, Assistant Secretary for the Near East and South Asia in the State Department, both of whom were my good friends. As I was informed, the meetings were scheduled for two separate days, the agenda for the first being the nuclear issue, and for the second the implementation of the Geneva Accords. At the first meeting, Zia looked us in the eye and said, 'We are not making such a weapon', and we knew that he was lying to us. At the second meeting, he told us that he intended to induct weapons into Afghanistan, and coolly dismissed our observation that it would be violating the Geneva Agreement that he had just signed. He said that 'Islam allowed him to lie for a good cause'. The Americans' correct and caustic comment was that 'on both occasions the [...] lied to us 'for the good cause of Islam'.

In December 1985, Martial Law in Pakistan was finally lifted, and political parties began to reorganize and resume their activities; the PPP in particular was galvanized by Benazir Bhutto's triumphant and rapturous return to the country, which had become weary after Zia's eight years of stifling puritanism. The politicians, who sensed this only too well, began to sharpen their knives as they cast their longing eyes on the ballot boxes. It occurred to me at the time that military rulers, even one as fearsome as Zia, have a limited shelf life: politicians, on the other hand, are a recyclable commodity. I recalled the words of my friend Abu Kureishi: 'Do not believe that any Pakistani politician is finished until you actually attend his *chehlum*' (fortieth-day prayers after death).

Zia, the consummate political manipulator, now found himself simultaneously engulfed in a series of major problems. The first was the prevailing turbulence within Pakistan, with the dismissal of Junejo and the return of Benazir Bhutto; the second was the increasing political hostility that prevailed in the US, with the Congress slapping on one sanction upon another over the nuclear issue; the third was the almost total lack of credibility in the US, as in Pakistan, over Zia's statements and actions. It was under the shadow of these dark clouds that it was decided to invite Zia to Washington on a 'working visit'. Protocol events, although not entirely excluded, were kept to the minimum, and the visit would be exclusively devoted to working sessions.

During my increasingly frequent visits to Islamabad, I noticed that the tensions in the country had begun to reflect in the drawing room of the Army House. I sensed also that Junejo's activities, coupled with time, had loosened Zia's grip on the administration, and that his touch was no longer as sure as it had been before. I left for Pakistan on 11 July 1988 for consultations on Zia's visit to Washington, for which the portents were more ominous than propitious. The dismissal of the Junejo government had created a far worse reaction in the US than I had imagined, and the view, especially in the Congress, was that of a rampant military dictatorship that could not tolerate even the façade of a democracy that had been its own creation. Furthermore, the promise of holding party-less elections was seen as akin to waving a very large red flag to an enraged bull. With the withdrawal of the Soviet forces from Afghanistan well underway, and due for completion by February, our hitherto heroic status as a frontline state in the international war for freedom had become, in the German idiom, *Schnee von gestern* (yesterday's snow).

Meanwhile, pressure on our nuclear programme was growing, and my discreet enquiries revealed that the US intelligence agencies were in complete accord that Pakistan had crossed the enrichment threshold and that the next certification was not only improbable, but impossible. Bearing these grim tidings, I arrived in Islamabad. The city was reeking with political uncertainty and an administration that seemed to have lost its touch. My meetings with senior officials such as Ghulam Ishaq Khan, Sahabzada Yaqub Khan, and Roedad Khan were reassuring in that they were aware of the serious nature of the problem and were prepared to deal with it realistically. They were not in the state of euphoric denial that has characterized so much of our political life.

My tight schedule permitted me only two days in Islamabad, the first of which was taken up by meetings at the Foreign Office (much hand-wringing on all sides). On the afternoon of the second day, I was to meet the President at the Aiwan-e-Sadr in Islamabad after he was through with his meetings with some political leaders, and then travel with him in his car to the Army House, conclude our discussions, and catch the evening flight back to New York.

I found Zia looking tired and haggard. Watching him from the waiting room of his office as he held discussions with political and religious leaders (mostly the latter), my mind went back to the days, almost a decade earlier, when Zulfikar Ali Bhutto was engaged in the same exercise with the same sort of people in the same atmosphere and location. Zia looked stressed, preoccupied, and fatigued in a manner that I had never seen. It was only when he came over and greeted me, smiling and courteous as ever, that I discerned a glimpse of the old Zia ul-Haq that I had known, respected, and had grown so fond of. As we drove from Islamabad to the Army House in a Toyota Corolla, there were no escorts, other than an army gunman seated next to the driver. I briefed Zia on the current situation in the United States and our relations with Washington, warning him that the situation was very different now. President Reagan and my wife Arnaz were likely to be the only friendly faces that he would see in the city. He should anticipate a moderate reception from the administration, a rough one from the Congress, and downright hostility from the media. Zia took all this in his usual cool manner, and we moved on to discuss the available options. I could see that Zia was looking forward to his Washington visit, but was doing so in a combative spirit and not one of pleasurable anticipation as had been the case before. There was anxiety in his questions and his body language, battered as he was by a succession of political blows. He appeared bruised and was no longer the coiled spring within a crisp *achkan* or uniform. But his mind was as sharp as ever, and he exuded his usual calm courage as we war-gamed the pattern of the forthcoming Washington visit. As I took my leave, Zia was his gracious self, asking me to convey his greetings to my wife, and thanking me for my services to Pakistan. He assured me that he would be in touch with me via telephone and was looking forward to our meeting in Washington. Fate decreed that this would be my last meeting with this great, admirable, courageous patriot.

Back in Washington, with the date for the visit fast approaching, I found myself in telephonic contact with Zia on an almost daily basis. Since these calls came at midday in Washington, I avoided all official lunches and had my meals with the telephone close to the table in my dining room. On the morning of 17 August 1988, I received in my office an urgent phone call from US Under Secretary Mike Armacost, seeking confirmation about an alarming report that he had just received about a plane crash in which both President Zia ul-Haq and US Ambassador Arnold Raphel had been killed. I immediately got through to Foreign

Secretary Humayun Khan in Islamabad, and he confirmed the worst. There followed the expected rush of activities and a flurry of telephone calls, including one by my dining table. Instinctively, I dashed to pick up the instrument, then realized with despair that the caller at the other end could not possibly be Zia ul-Haq ...

I was told that, on hearing of Zia's death, Charlie Wilson, the rambunctious, hard-boiled Congressman from Texas and Zia's great friend and admirer, shut himself in his office and wept for the whole day.

Two Prime Ministers assassinated; One Prime Minister hanged; One President blown up.

10

Ghulam Ishaq Khan: 1988–1993

A Prophet is not without honour except in his home.

The Holy Bible

Little monk, little monk, you have chosen a difficult path.

Cautionary advice to Martin Luther when he chose to enter politics
by deciding to attend the Diet of Worms in 1521.

Ghulam Ishaq Khan was the consummate civil servant,
and probably one of the three best administrators I knew
that Pakistan ever had: the other two were Chaudhry
Muhammad Ali and G. Ahmed. But the similarity does not
end there. Ghulam Ishaq Khan and Chaudhry Muhammad
Ali, at the end of their brilliant careers as administrators,
entered the uncharted field of politics, where they achieved
brief success at the top as heads of state/government, but
ended their respective administrations in comparatively
undistinguished fashion. Their performance as politicians
by no means matched their achievements as administrators.
The main reason, as I perceived it in the case of Ghulam
Ishaq Khan, was his discomfort at having to function in the
hurly-burly of politics. A highly intelligent, quiet, dignified,
and reserved man, he was incapable of raising his voice even
in normal conversation, let alone addressing a crowd. He
was much more comfortable (and effective) when disposing

off files on his desk, or participating in conferences wherein his knowledge, powers of expression, and presentation could be used to devastating effect, in making a presentation or demolishing an opponent's argument.

Starting as a humble mid-level civil servant, he rose, through sheer dint of ability, industry, and intelligence, to become the President of Pakistan (1988). He was sustained in this remarkable career path by his total honesty, incorruptibility, and steely determination. Above all, he was blessed by the stroke of good fortune which, by timing and circumstance, has been the prerequisite for the path to success of so many statesmen. After meritorious and devoted service to Zia ul-Haq and his administration, Ghulam Ishaq, in expectation of a job carrying a high status and political power, was disappointed with his appointment as Chairman of the Senate, a largely ceremonial post devoid of political clout. Just as we, his friends, met him to console him in his frustration and point out that there would still be opportunities for him to serve Pakistan, fate intervened. The fickle destiny that hurled President Zia ul-Haq to his death into the Bahawalpur desert (August 1988) also wafted Ghulam Ishaq Khan into the Aiwan-e-Sadr in Islamabad. Under the Constitution (framed by Zia), the Chairman of the Senate was the successor to the President.

In the dazed and confused situation that prevailed after the sudden death of Zia, it was reported that Ghulam Ishaq Khan met General Aslam Beg, the Vice Chief of Army Staff, and now COAS, to ascertain the views of the army, and whether there was any intention to declare

Martial Law. After consulting the senior generals, Beg told Ishaq Khan that the civil order should remain undisturbed. Accordingly, Ghulam Ishaq Khan became the President of Pakistan on 17 August 1988.

I first met Ghulam Ishaq Khan when he was a Member of the recently constituted Planning Commission, whose Chairman was the most able and versatile G. Ahmed. I was introduced to him by our common friend Roedad Khan, thus forming a trio that lasted a lifetime. Already, Ghulam Ishaq Khan had the reputation of being a high flyer, and I could immediately gauge why. Soft spoken and taciturn in manner, he literally radiated intelligence and ability. Coupled with this was a measure of intellectual arrogance and an undisguised inability to suffer fools gladly. In the course of time, as I worked with Ghulam Ishaq and got to know him better, my admiration for his intellectual brilliance increased exponentially, as it did for his determination, steadfastness, and patriotism. I vividly recall seeing him in the drawing room of his modest home, working on the files which surrounded him, as he listened to news and music from Radio Kabul, a station which, though not banned in Pakistan at that time, was nevertheless much frowned upon by officialdom. Although a workaholic, Ghulam Ishaq possessed a sardonic sense of humour and had no difficulty in abandoning his files for an informal little chat with friends, especially if the conversation was spiced with gossip; the more salacious, the better.

Since the subject of administration in Pakistan was better known to Ghulam Ishaq Khan than the contours on the back of his hand, he slipped smoothly into the duties of his office as soon as he had ascertained from General Aslam Beg that the army had opted for continuity. But this was the relatively easier course to follow in the path to succession. Zia ul-Haq had firmly concentrated in his hands Pakistan's essential priorities: the army, the nuclear issue, Afghanistan, India, and related foreign policy subjects. With his sudden disappearance, it appeared to outside observers like myself that there were new contenders for these important levers of power. The most important of these was Benazir Bhutto, who returned to Pakistan from exile in 1986. She was welcomed by thronging crowds. Following the death of Zia, on 16 November 1988 (the date previously set by Zia ul-Haq and later confirmed by Ghulam Ishaq Khan and General Aslam Beg), General Elections were held in Pakistan, and resulted in a victory for Benazir and her Pakistan Peoples Party (although not with absolute majority). There followed a hectic and desperate struggle for succession and power, the public aspect of which was known to us at the time, but I knew little of the process that eventually evolved the *troika* formula, with power shared between President, Prime Minister, and Army Chief. All that I could conclude was that Bhutto had conceded much real power in her obsession for the pomp of office.

On 1 December 1988, Benazir took the oath of office as Prime Minister of Pakistan, in the presence of her mother Nusrat Bhutto at a ceremony filled with euphoria and bittersweet emotion. Among her many other distinctions was that of being the first elected lady Prime Minister of an Islamic nation. Also, as I perceived it at the time, she was surrounded, in an atmosphere of simultaneous joy and uncertainty, by dubious friends and rivals in equal numbers.

Within the powerful army also, the process of change and succession had taken place. But this was done in an orderly fashion, as was usually the case with the army. In August 1991, General Aslam Beg was replaced by General Asif Nawaz. This was a popular choice, both in the country and the armed services, as he was a thorough professional, a true soldier's soldier, dedicated to keeping the army away from politics and concentrating on improving and honing its military capability. I met him when he visited New York shortly after he had taken over as COAS (we were still a Member of the Security Council) and accompanied him on his various meetings with UN officials and Ambassadors to the UN. He created an excellent impression, there being no doubt about his professional competence and his determination to keep the army out of politics in Pakistan. As I bade farewell to General Asif Nawaz at JFK airport in New York, I was grateful that we at last had a man of his calibre as our COAS. This feeling was soon shattered by the news of his sudden death from a heart attack in January 1993. The malign fates seemed determined to haunt the destiny of Pakistan.

As for Ghulam Ishaq Khan, armed with honesty, intellect, pen and paper, he was about to enter into terra incognita, where there was no shortage of knives and daggers. It became a matter of integrity or intrigue, and as events were to reveal, the latter prevailed. Perhaps the most prominent feature of Ghulam Ishaq's tenure was the notable manner in which he brought order and financial discipline into government, and the firm determination which characterized the implementation of his policies. But these same attributes, so essential for an administrator, prove to be damaging to a political leader, who needs flexibility in his conduct and approach.

During the time that I worked with Ghulam Ishaq, I remained in awe and admiration of his skills and determination. Without his capable handling of the issue, Pakistan would never have achieved the success in the nuclear field at the time that it did, and the country owes him an enormous debt of gratitude which has neither been acknowledged nor paid. On the other hand, his rigid economic shibboleths have stilted the growth of the country and left it mired in the neo-socialist morass of the state control system. Trained in the British colonial administrative system, adopted in the subcontinent from the United Kingdom's Atlee/Cripps government of post-World War II, Ghulam Ishaq maintained his fascination for rigidity and controls in all forms of administration, a policy that he imposed upon the country, so that the liberal impulses that blew over much of Asia following the technological revolution almost bypassed Pakistan.

The other major failure in Ghulam Ishaq's tenure was his inability to adapt to the political climate and mores of the Pakistan environment, and to operate within the confines of the system. Francis Bacon, in one of his essays, quotes the Roman historian and Senator Tacitus' observation on Galba (who was Roman Emperor for only seven months): *'omnium consensus capax imperii, nisi imperasset'* (had he never been Emperor all would have pronounced him fit for Empire). I frequently recalled this remark as I observed Ghulam Ishaq Khan stumble his way through the political morass of Pakistan, particularly in what was to be the final period of his Presidency.*

By now, Benazir Bhutto and Nawaz Sharif had entered the scene, which was evolving in its usual Byzantine fashion. The *troika* had become a game of musical chairs whose initial participants were Ghulam Ishaq Khan (President), Generals Aslam Beg and Asif Nawaz (Army Chiefs), and Benazir Bhutto (Prime Minister). Changes in its composition were brought about by the results of two elections, with Benazir being replaced by Nawaz Sharif (in 1990) and vice versa (Benazir became Prime Minister again in October 1993). The details of these convoluted events in Pakistan's internal political affairs are best left to history, some of which has already been recorded. I remained in New York during this period as Permanent Representative to the UN, being asked to do so by the President and the

---

*See *Crossed Swords: Pakistan, Its Army, and the Wars Within* by Shuja Nawaz (Karachi: Oxford University Press, 2008). A seminal work which, among other important issues, contains a succinct and lucid account of the manner in which Pakistan muddled its way through this particular murky spell in its troubled history. I am most grateful to the author for the guidelines which have been generously provided in the book, and which I have perused with great care and interest.

two succeeding Prime Ministers. But I naturally followed developments as closely as one could, with considerable anxiety.

Differences between President Ghulam Ishaq Khan and Prime Minister Benazir Bhutto were coming to a head, and from what I could tell from New York, there was much dirty work at the crossroads brewing in Islamabad. This only evoked in me feelings of contempt for each of the participants, with Ghulam Ishaq making overtures to Benazir for an association against Nawaz Sharif. Using his extraconstitutional powers, which had been allowed to the President through the Eighth Amendment, Ghulam Ishaq Khan dismissed Nawaz Sharif in April 1993. This resulted in an unholy alliance and the formation of a large Caretaker Government, under Balakh Sher Mazari, a political orphan, and including Asif Ali Zardari as Minister for Investment. Hence the poacher was turned gamekeeper, and Benazir had extracted her pound of flesh.

Admiration of Ghulam Ishaq Khan throughout the country turned into disbelief and disappointment bordering on contempt. He who hitherto regarded an impeccable hero was now perceived an opportunist, and a not too successful one at that. As I followed these developments from distant New York with helpless personal anguish, I felt that I was going back centuries in time and space, a witness on the bank of the Jhelum river watching Porus clinging to his swinging *howdah* perched on the back of his elephant, under ruthless attack by Alexander's conquering armies.

Given his sudden untimely death, General Asif Nawaz, the Chief of Army Staff, was greatly missed at this juncture. Fortunately, his successor, General Waheed Kakar, was cast in similar mould, a thorough professional with sound judgement and instincts. When the Supreme Court decided that the President's dismissal of Nawaz Sharif, under the Eighth Amendment, was *ultra vires*, Ghulam Ishaq was stunned, and the politics of Pakistan were once again in turmoil. Finally, in July 1993, General Waheed Kakar brokered an agreement, whereby, both Ghulam Ishaq Khan and Nawaz Sharif would resign, and an interim neutral government would be established, charged with holding elections within three months. This was the end of the *troika*.

Benazir and Nawaz Sharif went into the background to sharpen their knives for the battles that they correctly anticipated were forthcoming. General Kakar, in a gesture that was as honourable as it was unique, retired on the due date of retirement, which was January 1996. He refused all suggestions (some very persuasive) that he take an extension.

Ghulam Ishaq Khan went into a retirement that had been virtually forced upon him, spending his last lonely days in isolation and ill health, at his modest home in Peshawar. He had acquired no lands or palatial residences: patriotism and service to Pakistan had been his priorities. Unfortunately, this could not be said of some of his close relatives, whose acquisitive conduct had been widely noted and deplored and was a considerable blot on Ghulam Ishaq Khan's own clean escutcheon.

The sad duty of politics is to establish justice in a sinful world.

Reinhold Niebuhr

11

Moeenuddin Qureshi:
July 1993–November 1993

A BRIEF INTERREGNUM: POSITIVE DEVELOPMENTS

I remained at my post in New York throughout the duration of the political crisis as it unfolded in Pakistan, a Permanent Representative of a government whose continuity itself was at that time uncertain. In Islamabad, the search for a new president and prime minister naturally set off a flurry of political activity, spurred essentially by General Waheed Kakar, who had succeeded the late General Asif Nawaz as Chief of Army Staff. It consisted of the usual process of consultations amongst political leaders and the army, with names proposed and rejected. The final choice for prime minister was Moeenuddin Ahmad Qureshi, generally referred to as Moeen Qureshi. He had recently retired after a distinguished career at the World Bank, and was heading his own prosperous firm in the international financial sector. Because of this, and also for health reasons, Qureshi was initially reluctant to accept the assignment, but did so after some heavy persuasion, and was brought from Singapore, where he was on a business trip, by a special aircraft to Islamabad for the Swearing-in Ceremony.

He remained Prime Minister of Pakistan from July 1993 to October 1993.

Moeen was a brilliant economist who had been in the Planning Commission of Pakistan before he joined the World Bank, where he had a spectacular career which ended with his office as Senior Vice President. I had known Moeen for some time, but first worked with him circa 1966, when I was Pakistan High Commissioner to Ghana in Accra. After the fall of Nkrumah, the new government was anxious to improve relations with the west, and a vital part of this exercise was to seek the support of international financial institutions. Moeen Qureshi was accordingly posted to Accra as the World Bank Representative to Ghana, with the daunting brief of clearing up the economic mess created by the Nkrumah regime, and establishing a sound economic and political structure in the country. Moeen went about his job in his usual effective, low-key manner, and achieved his objectives within a few months, turning a sick state into a near vibrant one. In the meantime, we got to know each other very well and established a firm lifelong friendship. Moeen was an urbane and sophisticated personality, highly intelligent and self-assured; qualities that earned him international recognition at the highest level. At a meeting in Singapore, when we were discussing East Timor, Lee Kuan Yew digressed from the subject to tell me that in his congratulatory message to Nawaz Sharif after the latter had become Prime Minister, he had included the suggestion, 'My advice is to continue the policies of Moeen Qureshi'.

On assuming office, Moeen wasted no time. He established a Cabinet of competent and dedicated professionals. I cannot recall all the names, but members included Syed Babar Ali as Finance Minister, Chaudhry Muhammad Farooq as Minister for Communications, and Khursheed Marker as Minister for Water and Power. Being an entrepreneur, Khursheed had been accustomed to working long hours, but he told me that he had never worked as hard in the private sector as he was obliged to do as a minister. But then, he had never been a politician either, and was also burdened with a far greater conscience than any of his predecessors or successors.

The task allotted to the Qureshi government was to achieve, within a three-month time frame, national political and economic stability, and then to hold free and fair elections. The newly installed Cabinet went about its job with determination, and enthusiasm, stepping on some toes in the process. For example, on taking over, Qureshi found a large number of financial defaulters (mostly unpaid or wrongly written off loans) and was compelled to reveal the list, since this included many prominent members of Nawaz Sharif's party, he was obviously angered. Nevertheless, the government proceeded with its reforms, perhaps the most important being the strengthening of the role of the State Bank of Pakistan, freeing it from supervision and control by the Finance Ministry and making it the independent institution that it always should have been.

Moeen came on a working visit to the US while I was still Permanent Representative at New York, and instructed me to accompany him to Washington. The Ambassador's post had been vacant for a while and I had been carrying out a holding operation to counter some very vigorous lobbying by Indian diplomats in their attempts to have Pakistan labelled as a terrorist state. As Moeen did the rounds of the power elite in Washington, all of whom were either his personal friends or knew of his capabilities, I was convinced that not only was the once dangerous bogey of being labelled a terrorist state laid to rest, but that support in full measure from the United States government was assured.

Moeen fulfilled the next condition of his obligation, and a very important one, i.e. holding elections on 27 October 1993. These were completely free and fair, and resulted in a win for the PPP, which secured 86 Muslim seats compared to PML-N's 77. Significantly, the Islamic parties when combined won very few seats, and the MQM none. Having fulfilled his commitment to the nation, Moeen dissolved his Cabinet and handed over power to Benazir Bhutto. Within the time constraints of his three-month tenure, this consummate political administrator had probably achieved as much for Pakistan as any of his predecessor Prime Ministers. Here Macaulay's observation of John Hampden comes to mind: 'The celebrated Puritan leader is an almost solitary instance of a great man who neither sought nor claimed greatness, who found glory only because glory lay in the path of duty'.

12

Benazir Bhutto:
1988–1990; 1993–1996

REDUX AND RESUME

Beauty, courage, and determination in abundance, tempered by acquisitiveness and incompetence. Devastated by the personal disasters that have always lurked in the stars of the Bhuttos.

My association with Benazir Bhutto became increasingly peripheral as she and her close advisers negotiated their way into a return to power. It terminated on both the occasions that she became Prime Minister (1988–1990; 1993–1996), with the resignations that I always submitted at the change of government. In this instance, there were two additional factors that motivated my action. One was my reservations with regard to Benazir's style and management of government, not to mention her choice of collaborators, who, when combined together, created a strong odour of incompetence and corruption. The other was my conviction that any Pakistan Ambassador to Washington, as I then was, must have direct access to and possess the confidence of the Head of Government. In my case, this was clearly not so. Accordingly, I submitted my letter of resignation, and offered to remain at my post till the conclusion of the Prime Minister's forthcoming visit, suggesting also that she include my successor in her delegation. Benazir was kind enough to accept both my suggestions, bringing with her the excellent choice of Air Chief Marshal Zulfikar Ali Khan. She accepted my resignation with a gracious observation: 'I should like to place on record the Government's appreciation of the valuable service you have rendered to your country during a record spell as Ambassador. You have served with distinction in some of the most important countries and often at difficult times.'

The preparatory work for the prime ministerial visit involved calls by a plethora of officials from Pakistan, who stayed on and joined the group of ministers, governors, and 'advisers' (hangers-on, freeloaders, and friends of friends) who, together, constituted one of the largest 'delegations' from Pakistan to visit the United States. Since Washington's invitation for an official visit is limited to only ten persons, including chief guest and spouse and ambassador and spouse, the tab for the rest was picked up, without prior knowledge or consent, by Pakistan's taxpayers. Nevertheless, Benazir's visit to the United States was a succès fou, and included an address to a Joint Session of the Senate and House of the United States Congress, and highly productive meetings with important individuals in the establishment ('We must do something for the lady'). Above all, she achieved a major success when she obtained the release of some F-16 fighter aircraft for which we had paid, but which had been seized by the sanctions imposed under the US nuclear embargo.

There now followed a plethora of visitors from Washington to Islamabad, all expressing goodwill and support for the Benazir government. These included everyone from influential Senators such as Daniel Patrick Moynihan to sturdy workhorses such as Peter Galbraith. And always there was Mark Siegel, a sinister and greedy American lobbyist who had been Benazir's friend and admirer for years. During this period, I was astonished to note the accessibility accorded to the Americans as they attended the meetings at the Prime Minister's office and participated in the preparation of briefs for her forthcoming official visit to the United States. Even subjects as sensitive as the nuclear issue were raised in the discussions. It became clear to me (with a barely concealed sense of relief) that the Prime Minister was not fully aware of the nuances of the situation. That old Pathan tiger, Ghulam Ishaq Khan, had kept it under close lock and key, and was guarding the contents like the fierce watchdog that he always was. At later meetings, which I was required to attend, I discovered that the American intelligence were playing the same games, also revealing to Benazir, on a reciprocal basis of selectivity, just as much or as little as they thought she should know. During her bilateral meetings with President George Bush, National Security Adviser General Brent Scowcroft, and Director of CIA Judge Webster, the topic was the same: dire warnings from the Americans about our nuclear programme, supported by some irrefutable evidence about its progress, and a total, but entirely understandable disbelief in our denials. We were both lying to each other and knew it. And always, there was the issue of nuclear enrichment as the Ancient Mariner with the albatross hanging around his neck, making his woeful presence felt at the wedding party.

To sum up, I thought that the Americans' attitude to Benazir was, like that of so many of us others, an amalgam of delight and distrust. When Prime Minister Benazir Bhutto departed from Washington at the conclusion of her official visit to the United States, and with my resignation from the government, all my contacts with Benazir had come to an end. But as an interested observer who had until so recently been associated with the ongoing events, I was naturally keen to follow them as closely as I could. At home, there were serious and urgent problems: those arising from the differences between Benazir and the upright and professional General Jehangir Karamat, the new Chief of Army Staff; and between Benazir and the new President, Farooq Ahmed Khan Leghari, an old and trusted PPP stalwart. Added to these was the perpetual issue of corruption, which was rife in the party at its highest level. To an appalled observer like myself, it was obvious that these matters were being mishandled by the Prime Minister in an inept Byzantine manner.

A further complication in Benazir's life was the notorious feud between her husband Asif Ali Zardari and her brother Murtaza Bhutto, culminating in the messy death of the latter in 1996. Coming so soon after the equally messy death of her other brother Shahnawaz (d.1985), in the immediate aftermath of a stormy public family dispute, one could only contemplate with apprehension the curse that prevailed upon the Bhuttos. How much of this was self-induced, and how much could be attributed to malign fate?

I never became close enough to Benazir to be considered either a friend or a beneficiary, but my professional association with her left me with impressions that have remained unaltered over time. In the first place, she had unbounded courage—'gutsy' would be the word—which would shine through during the worst periods of many of her personal crises. Her last two public speeches, when she accused and challenged the Taliban, were amongst the greatest acts of daring and political courage ever displayed in Pakistan. They were delivered during a time of high tension, livened by threats of all kinds, including assassination. But she chose to ignore these and, like Joan of Arc, courageously marched to meet her cruel end. The word *Shaheed* (martyr) has been so frequently used in Pakistan that it has become almost as meaningless as most of the Civil Awards accorded by the government to its favourites on Pakistan Day. In the case of Benazir, who consciously and deliberately forfeited her life as she passionately warned her countrymen of the evils and horrors of fundamentalism, there is no titular description other than *Shaheed*.

Benazir possessed abundant charm, which she knew how to blend with her femininity as she worked without scruple on the object of her attention. I have emerged from meetings with her, both individual and collective, where to me her duplicitous intentions and objectives were quite evident, and yet there was the urge to slay dragons and lay them at her feet. Dealing with Benazir was as tricky as trying to handle Eve and the Serpent at the same time.

Needless to say, there is always the compulsion to compare Benazir with her father Zulfikar Ali Bhutto (ZAB). My view, on the limited basis of having worked with both of them, is that whilst there was nothing to choose between them in terms of arrogance, amorality, and lack of scruple, ZAB was far superior in intelligence than his daughter. But in the end, their fates decreed equality in the manner of their death—both met with premature and violent deaths.

NOTE

1. See, *Quiet Diplomacy* by Jamsheed Marker (Karachi: Oxford University Press, 2010), 286–7.

13

Mian Muhammad Nawaz Sharif:
1990–1993; 1997–1999

THE MARKET PLACE ENTERS THE TEMPLE

I first met Mian Nawaz Sharif in the summer of 1982. It was shortly after I had presented credentials in Paris, and established what were later to become very close relations with François de Grossouvre, the influential Special Assistant to President François Mitterrand. He had, at that time, been on an official visit to Pakistan, and my wife Arnaz and I were designated to escort him and his wife during their stay in the country.

I met Mian Nawaz Sharif for the first time in Lahore—he was at that time the Finance Minister of Punjab and had been nominated as Minister-in-Waiting to de Grossouvre for his visit to Punjab. It was common belief at the time that not only was Nawaz a protégé of the Punjab Governor, General Ghulam Jilani Khan, but that his pedigree also possessed the warm endorsement of President Zia ul-Haq. (I was therefore, in a sense, beginning my relationships with Zia's political grandson!) Fair and chubby of visage, energetic and hospitable, Nawaz gave us a warm and friendly reception. But since he did not bring up any political issues or matters relating to the Punjab, and de Grossouvre appeared equally disinclined for serious discussion, the conversation was restricted to pleasantries. Nawaz talked about the lunch and de Grossouvre discussed the boar hunt.

A shoot was arranged for de Grossouvre. It became clear to me there that Nawaz was deeply involved in the politics of the Punjab and remained in intensive discussions on the subject with the companions who had accompanied him on the shoot. The presence of the VIP French guest could not have been more peripheral. Even as I deplored this lack of manners on the part of Nawaz, I committed my own breach of etiquette by overhearing his conversation with his fellow politicians. It left me impressed. Apart from a lively interest in politics, which now seemed to precede his considerable business interests, Nawaz appeared to be preparing himself for a spring from provincial minister to something higher at the national level.

Over time, my interactions with Nawaz increased, largely because of our common association with the Governor of Punjab, General Ghulam Jilani Khan, who was an old and dear friend, having been with me at the Doon School, Dehradun. But this association with Nawaz remained largely on a pleasant social level, because even though Nawaz, after he became Prime Minister, had reappointed me as Permanent Representative to the UN, there was not much occasion for personal contact. Nawaz was kind enough to let me know that he reposed his confidence in me. Hence, for the first few months of my tenure, I was in the happy position of seeing my recommendations to government coming back to me as instructions.

In 1992, Pakistan was elected Chairman of the Group of 77 at the United Nations in New York. One result of it was that we had to play an important role at the United Nations Conference on Environment and Development (UNCTAD) at Rio de Janeiro in July 1992. Nawaz arrived as head of an enormous delegation of mostly freeloaders. They took full advantage of the salubrious air of Rio, explored and exploited its other attractions, and therefore happily did not interfere with us in our work. Nawaz spent some time in bilateral meetings with his counterparts, and also generally followed the guidelines that we had prepared in our script for the UNCTAD meetings. His attention, during his short stay in Rio, remained devoted to issues other than environment and development, but I noticed, in the few bilateral meetings that I attended with him, that the span of his attention remained as short as ever. This was an unfortunate characteristic of Nawaz that caused caution in my relations with him throughout our association, but I also knew that he could be quick and decisive if the subject interested him, or more particularly, if it had a personal pecuniary attraction.

After the Rio de Janeiro Conference, my visits to Pakistan became infrequent, and so did my meetings with Nawaz Sharif. But I did have the opportunity to follow from a distance the political developments in Islamabad, with all the intrigues and infighting in the National Assembly, among the political parties, and even the courts. These resulted in the changes of governments and prime ministers, with the carousel ending in early December 1997 when Nawaz Sharif became Prime Minister for the second time, following a large electoral majority. In the meantime, there had been major changes in the leadership of the armed forces. In January 1993, General Abdul Waheed Kakar became COAS following the untimely death of General Asif Nawaz Janjua, and was duly succeeded in January 1996 by General Jehangir Karamat. All three of them were upright professionals. In my short visits to Islamabad during this period, I could not help noticing the contrast between the smooth transition in the army, and the messy wheeling and dealing that was simultaneously in process in the National and Provincial Assemblies.

The most important concern at that time was the nuclear issue. India had just tested five nuclear bombs, which not only placed Pakistan under tremendous domestic pressure to respond, but also placed it under equal counter-pressure by the US, through the usual combination of threats and inducements, to 'take the high moral ground' and refrain from nuclear testing. I was in Islamabad at the moment when Nawaz was confronted with this dilemma, and although he appeared to be veering towards the option of nuclear testing, I felt compelled to encourage him to do so. In my view, this would provide an effective counter-check to the existing imbalance in Indo-Pak conventional forces, which in turn could help in the establishment of peace in the subcontinent. This was on the lines of the NATO/Warsaw Pact accommodation (MAD, Mutual

Assured Destruction) which had held the peace in Europe for a number of years. In the event, Nawaz needed no encouragement, and went ahead to test six nuclear weapons (one more than India), duly encountering the wrath (and sanctions) of President Clinton. In a staff conference later on (at which I was not present), I was told that Nawaz was euphoric about the testing, and confident that he would ride out the consequences. He was probably right on both counts.

It was at this time that I left the Pakistan Foreign Service and assumed my post in the United Nations. Another series of tumultuous days in Pakistani politics began, but I was out of the country at the time, on my United Nations assignment on East Timor, and therefore had no direct contact with Nawaz Sharif. But I followed with interest both his domestic and external political activities. These included the commendable visit of the Indian Prime Minister Atal Bihari Vajpayee to Lahore in 1999, and the deplorable military action in Kargil in 1999, necessitating a panic flight to Washington and a severe reprimand by President Bill Clinton prior to his intercession to end the conflict (and the changes in the army command structures leading to the fateful appointment of General Pervez Musharraf as Army Chief in 1998).

My personal association with Mian Nawaz Sharif was always productive and pleasant. His knowledge and comprehension of international affairs remained limited, and although he was also a slow learner, he was neither opinionated nor arrogant. His political inclination reflected

a pious conservative, rather than a deeply religious background. He maintained his businessman's instinct for
the practical, as he frequently demonstrated during the
early phase of his political career. Although he had been
piloted to political eminence by the military (Generals Zia
ul-Haq and Ghulam Jilani Khan), he claimed to have cast
off this cloak, and relished presenting himself in his new
role as an enterprising industrialist who had taken over
Punjab politics and replaced the old landowning class of
conservatives. If I noticed this transformation, I noticed
also, with considerable regret, that many of the old habits
die hard, and tales of corruption and cronyism in the new
regime were not only widespread but amply justified.
The increase in the acquisition of property and assets of
the Nawaz Sharif family was epitomized in the opulent
estate at Raiwind, which stood as a dismal addition to the
legend of corruption in Pakistan. The contest between the
Bhutto/Zardari dynasty and the Nawaz Sharif dynasty in
the realm of corruption is a close-run thing. It is difficult
to tell the difference, especially as the methods and devices
of acquisition and concealment in both cases are similar.

I was still living abroad when Nawaz Sharif was navigating
his way through the murky politics of Pakistan. But I was
able to note, with immense satisfaction, two achievements
that had a profound beneficial effect on the country.
Both were the result of bold decisions. The first was to
remove foreign exchange restrictions and to allow Pakistan
unfettered admission and entrance into the international
financial market. The second, related measure was to make

Pakistan a free-market economy, which meant releasing the economy from the coils of the restrictive bureaucracy that had for years enthusiastically imposed crippling regulations on the country. Unfortunately, here too, this commendable legislation was later sullied by an administrative measure that expropriated all foreign currency holdings in Pakistan banks in exchange for Pakistani rupees at the prevalent depreciated rate. This highly reprehensible arbitrary act aroused tremendous outrage within the country and abroad (I happened to be one of the victims) and led to an international loss of confidence in Pakistan, from which the country has not yet recovered. The official reason for this national financial penalty was that it was a necessity compelled by the US imposition of sanctions following the nuclear tests made by us. We were urged to accept this sacrifice and tighten our belts as a patriotic duty, and many of us did. However, an incriminating aspect of the episode was the rumour that the top leaders of the country (Sharif family and friends?), with foreknowledge of the regulation, had already closed their foreign exchange accounts and remitted the proceeds abroad. The rumour is still persistent, and I for one still have a lurking suspicion that it is true.

In the summer of 1999, relations between Pakistan and India, which had hitherto shown promise of improvement, took a nosedive after the Kargil conflict. I was still at the United Nations in New York, and could only look askance at the developments in the subcontinent. Almost as disturbing, at this distance, were the reports that were filtering through about differences that were emerging between the Prime Minister and the Chief of Army Staff. This was by no means unprecedented, and Rawalpindi and Islamabad, though in close geographic proximity, have frequently been far apart in terms of ideological and political priorities. This was the case in the autumn of 1999, when matters came to a head with the drama of the 'hijacking' of General Pervez Musharraf's aircraft and the consequent arrest of Nawaz Sharif, followed by his trial and exile to Saudi Arabia. A short, sharp conflict had clearly left Musharraf as winner and Nawaz Sharif as loser.

When you strike at a king, you must kill him.

Ralph Waldo Emerson

14

General Pervez Musharraf: 1999–2008

When can their glory fade?
O the wild charge they made!
All the world wondered!

Tennyson: Charge of the Light Brigade

C'est magnifique, mais ce n'est pas la guerre.
(It's magnificent, but it isn't war.)

Le Marechal Bosquet, French observer
at the charge of the Light Brigade at Balaclava

My first meeting with General Pervez Musharraf was in 1994, when, as Major General and Director General of Military Operations, he had organized a United Nations Peacekeeping Conference at the GHQ (General Headquarters) in Rawalpindi. Pakistan had always been a major troop contributor to the UN peacekeeping force, and General Musharraf had shown commendable initiative in convening this meeting and inviting senior representatives from the major troop-contributing nations to this conference. As I happened to be Pakistan's Permanent Representative to the United Nations at the time, and also President of the Security Council, I was invited to attend the seminar and preside over its deliberations. I was impressed not only by the organization of the meetings, but also by General Musharraf's participation in the discussions. Subsequently, we developed a friendly rapport.

My next contact with Musharraf was in October 1999. He had just 'taken over as Chief Executive'—an euphemism for martial law that fooled no one—and was in the process of forming his Cabinet. I was in New York at the time, winding up my UN association over East Timor, when I received a telephone call from Musharraf inviting me to join his government, despite the fact that hitherto our association had been limited to the brief two-week UN seminar on peacekeeping in Islamabad. For a variety of reasons, I was unable to accept his kind offer of a permanent assignment, but was appointed as Ambassador-at-Large, provided with a diplomatic passport, and served in an honorary capacity as Adviser on Foreign Affairs. As a result, I was a member of the Pakistan delegation to a number of United Nations conferences, had several meetings with the President during my visits to Pakistan, and went on to develop a personal and family relationship with him.

The impressions that I gathered about Musharraf, since my first association with him, circa early 2000, have remained more or less the same, except perhaps with an increase in feelings of friendship through the passage of time. Initially, it was his forceful and forthright demeanour that came to my attention. Later, as I got to know him better, there was the unmistakable evidence of an inclination to strike first and think afterwards, perhaps acceptable in a soldier, but much less so in a statesman. Above all, I was struck by the messianic zeal which seemed to characterize his attitude towards life in general, and towards Pakistan in particular. For me, an impartial assessment of Musharraf and his achievement is hampered by two elements: (a) personal regard; and (b) closeness of time. When asked for his views on the French Revolution (1789), the Chinese Premier Zhou En-lai had famously responded, 'it is too soon to say'. Similarly, I feel compelled to exercise restraint in the case of Musharraf. Though perhaps not waiting for three centuries, one might venture a preliminary assessment of his major accomplishments and failures. As so often happens, the major successes took place during the early period of Musharraf's administration, and the failures (some of them quite disastrous and leading to his downfall) took place later.

Musharraf's initial successes were in the realm of law and order, and in recouping Pakistan's financial and economic situation, increasing GDP growth from US$63 billion to US$170 billion (with a 7 per cent annual growth rate), and foreign exchange reserves from US$0.5 billion in 1999 to US$16.5 billion in 2008. For the same period, revenue generation grew from Rs. 308 million to Rs. 1 trillion. Similar advances were made in the agricultural, educational, and power generation sectors. But perhaps the most dramatic changes came in the media and communications fields, where the increase in fibre-optic activity and the induction of the cell phone created a virtual social revolution in the country. He gave freedom to the media that gave rise to the burgeoning of private television channels.

As time went by, and I got to know Musharraf better through our occasional work together, I was impressed by the basic decency of the man and also by his fervent (though sometimes misplaced, as in Kargil) patriotism. Despite the impression created from reading his (ghost-written) autobiography, he was basically devoid of arrogance in his daily conduct. In the first years of his administration, Pakistan enjoyed a period of stability and economic progress that it had not known for a long time. With these heady changes, every military ruler eventually has the urge to seek political legitimacy, a desire that is fuelled by the enthusiastic encouragement of the sycophantic coterie of flatterers that attach themselves to leaders, especially Pakistani leaders. It is my surmise that it was this factor, coupled with a fixation to hold on to power at any cost, that led Musharraf into committing the two primary errors (blunders would be the more appropriate expression) that brought about his downfall. The first of these was his conflict with the Chief Justice of Pakistan, Iftikhar Muhammad Chaudhry, rightly provoked and deserved, in my view. But the brutal manner of his dismissal invoked public outrage. This was the first public demonstration against Musharraf. The second error of Musharraf was the promulgation of the National Reconciliation Ordinance (NRO) on 5 October 2007. It was an infamous item of legislation that sanctified every political crime in the book, and 'honourably' liberated every person associated with it including Benazir Bhutto and Asif Ali Zardari. (The fates decree that the aftermath of both hubris and nemesis can be equally stark and dramatic.)

The rest, as the saying goes, is history. It is a history that is continuing to evolve, and one for future historians to record.

Index